MAX AXIOM AND THE SOCIETY OF SUPER SCIENTISTS

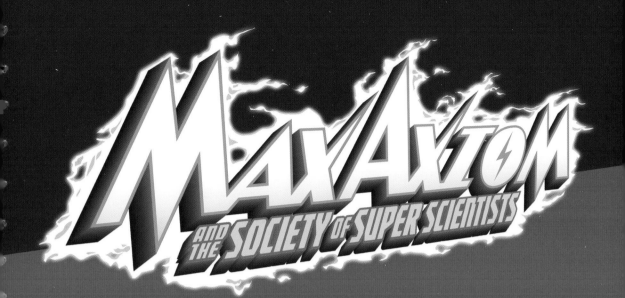

GLOBAL WATER CRISIS

BY MYRA FAYE TURNER
ILLUSTRATED BY ERIK DOESCHER

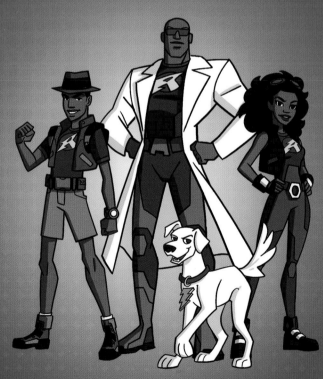

CAPSTONE PRESS
a capstone imprint

Published by Capstone Press, an imprint of Capstone.
1710 Roe Crest Drive
North Mankato, Minnesota 56003
capstonepub.com

Library of Congress Cataloging-in-Publication Data
Names: Turner, Myra Faye, author. | Doescher, Erik, illustrator.
Title: Global water crisis : a max axiom super scientist adventure /
  Myra Faye Turner ; illustrated by Erik Doescher.
Description: North Mankato, Minnesota : Capstone Press, [2022] |
  Series: Max axiom and the society of super scientists | Includes
  bibliographical references and index. | Audience: Ages 8-11 |
  Audience: Grades 4-6
Summary: "More than 70 percent of Earth is covered in water. Yet only
  about 3 percent of it is freshwater that people can use. Every year, parts
  of the world suffer through severe droughts, and millions of people
  don't have easy access to clean drinking water. Why is there a shortage
  of clean and healthy water? In this nonfiction graphic novel, Max Axiom
  and the Society of Super Scientists travel around the world to learn the
  reasons behind the global water crisis. Young readers can tag along to
  discover what causes water scarcity and find out ways they can help
  preserve this precious resource"-- Provided by publisher.
Identifiers: LCCN 2021029722 (print) | LCCN 2021029723 (ebook) |
  ISBN 9781663959195 (hardcover) | ISBN 9781666322682 (paperback) |
  ISBN 9781666322699 (pdf) | ISBN 9781666322712 (kindle edition)
Subjects: LCSH: Water supply--Juvenile literature. | Drinking water--
  Juvenile literature.
Classification: LCC TD348 .T87 2022 (print) | LCC TD348 (ebook) |
  DDC 363.6/1--dc23
LC record available at https://lccn.loc.gov/2021029722
LC ebook record available at https://lccn.loc.gov/2021029723

Editorial Credits
Editor: Aaron Sautter; Designer: Brann Garvey; Media Researcher:
Morgan Walters; Production Specialist: Laura Manthe

All internet sites appearing in back matter were available and accurate
when this book was sent to press.

TABLE OF CONTENTS

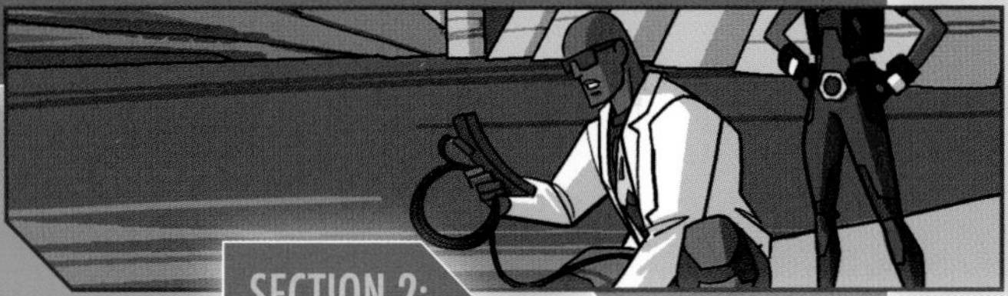

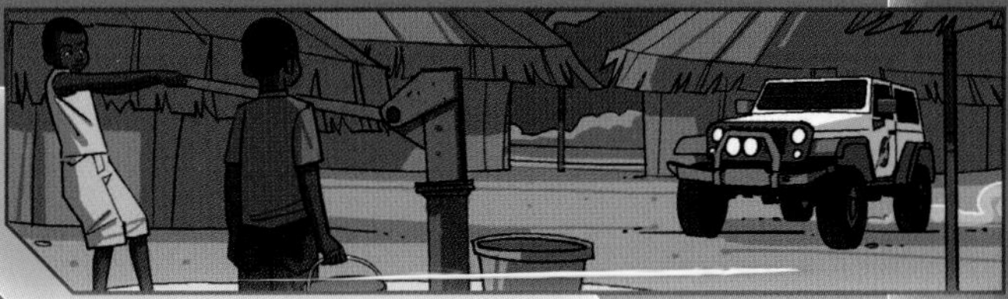

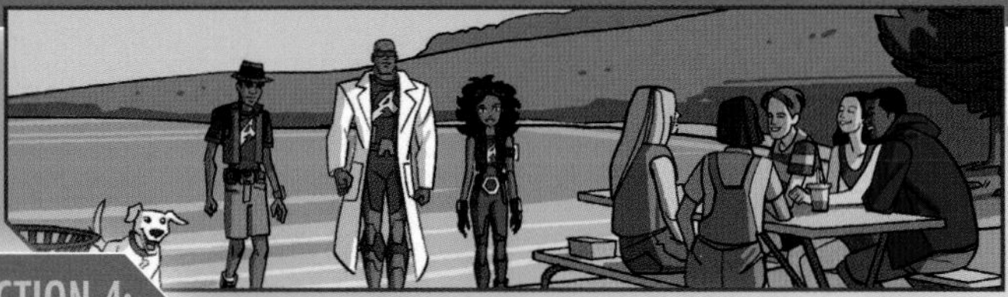

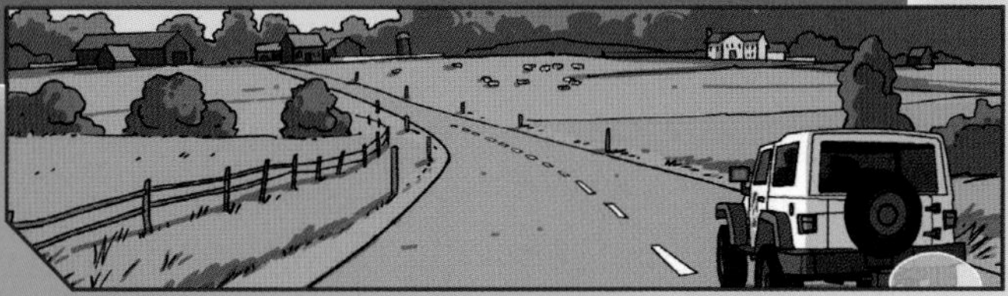

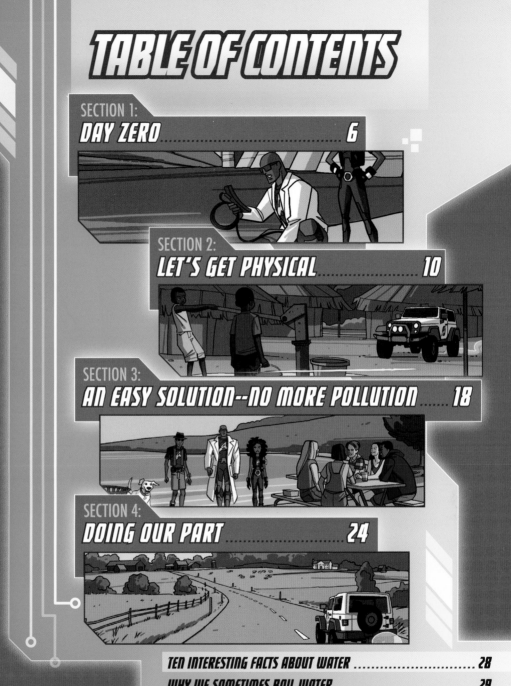

THE SOCIETY OF SUPER SCIENTISTS

MAX AXIOM

After years of study, Max Axiom, the world's first Super Scientist, knew the mysteries of the universe were too vast for one person alone to uncover. So Max created the Society of Super Scientists! Using their superpowers and super-smarts, this talented group investigates today's most urgent scientific and environmental issues and learns about actions everyone can take to solve them.

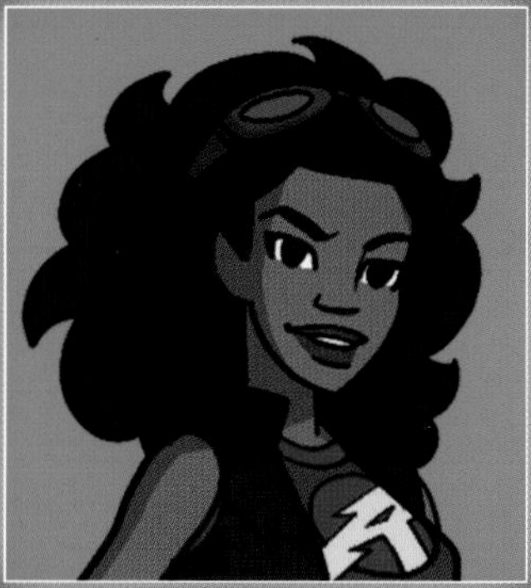

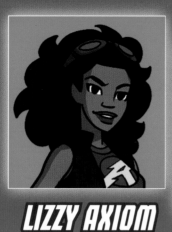

LIZZY AXIOM

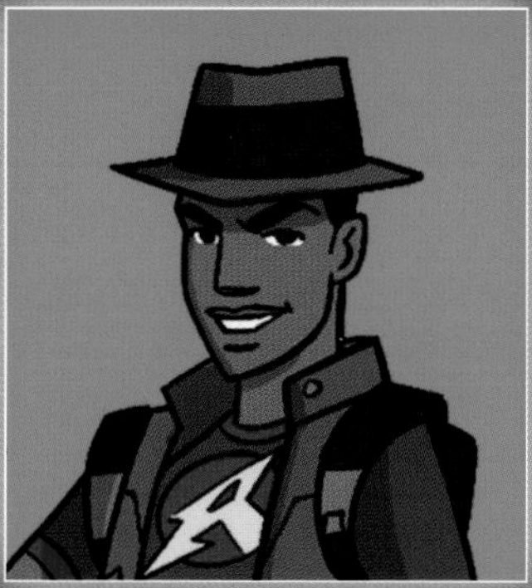

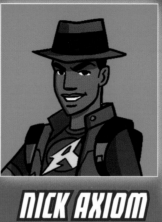

NICK AXIOM

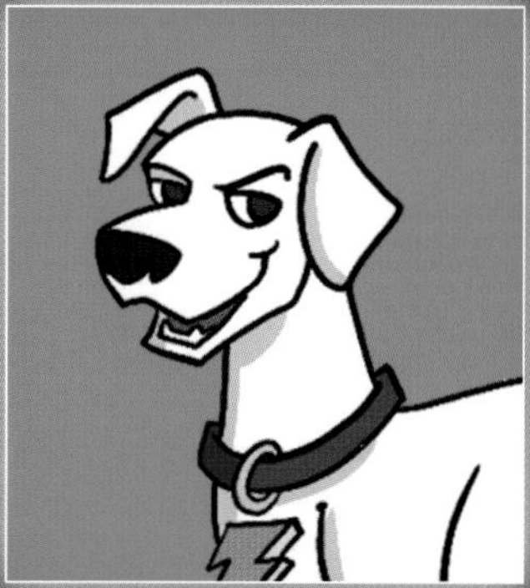

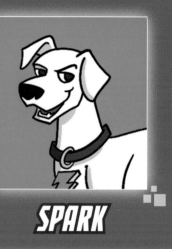

SPARK

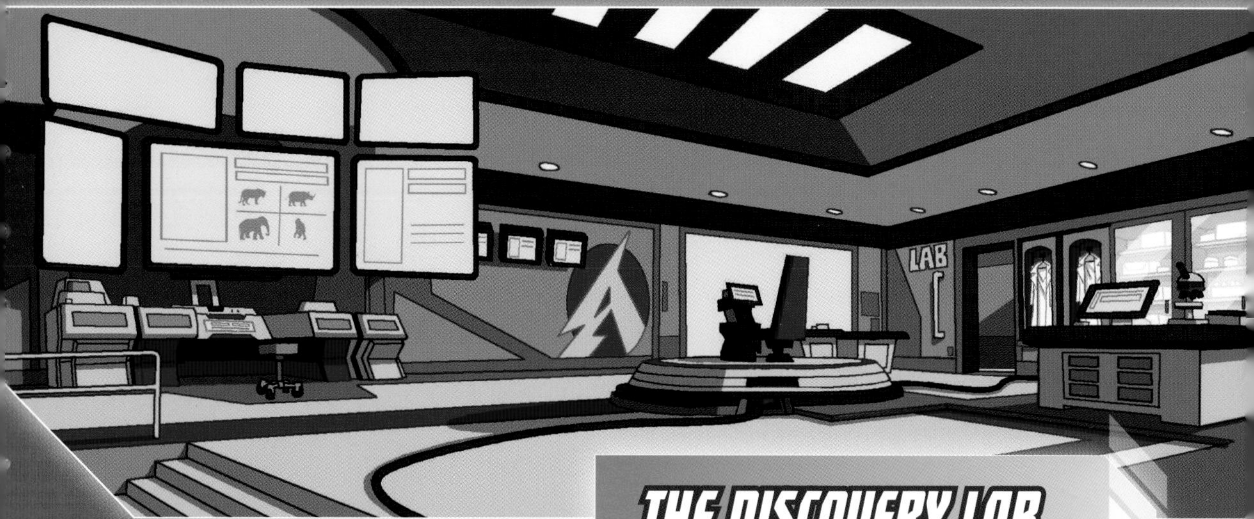
LAB

THE DISCOVERY LAB

Home of the Society of Super Scientists, this state-of-the-art lab houses advanced tools for cutting-edge research and radical scientific innovation. More importantly, it is a space for Super Scientists to collaborate and share knowledge as they work together to tackle any challenge.

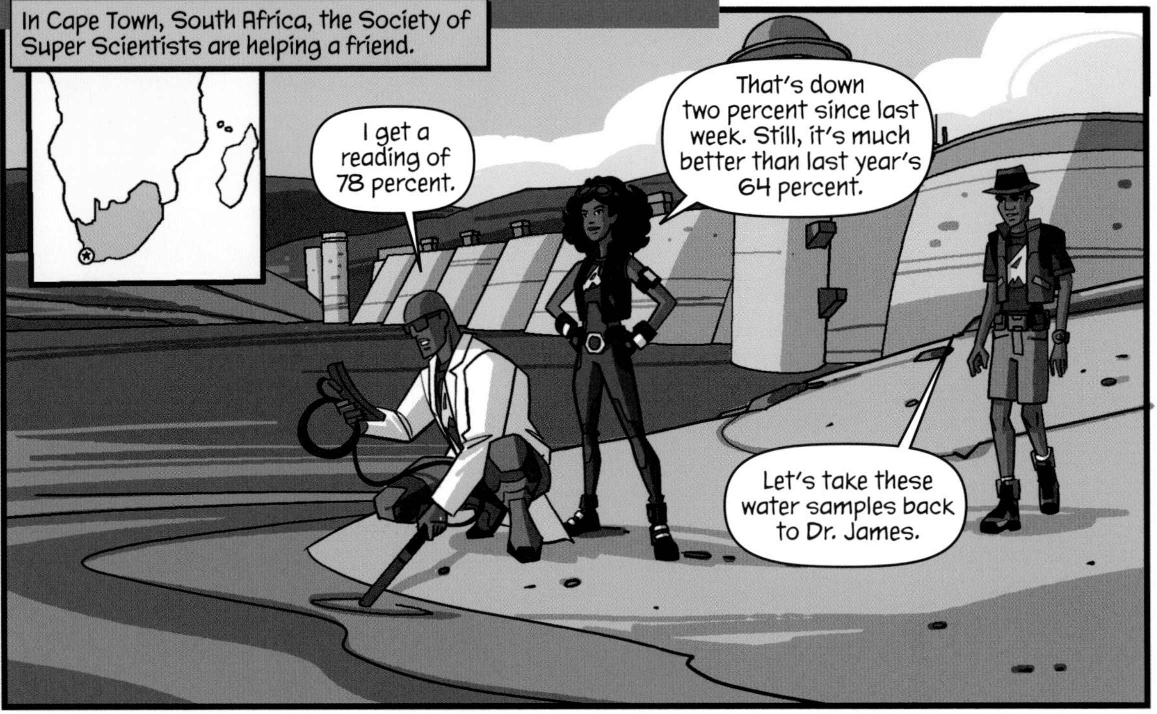
In Cape Town, South Africa, the Society of Super Scientists are helping a friend.
I get a reading of 78 percent.
That's down two percent since last week. Still, it's much better than last year's 64 percent.
Let's take these water samples back to Dr. James.

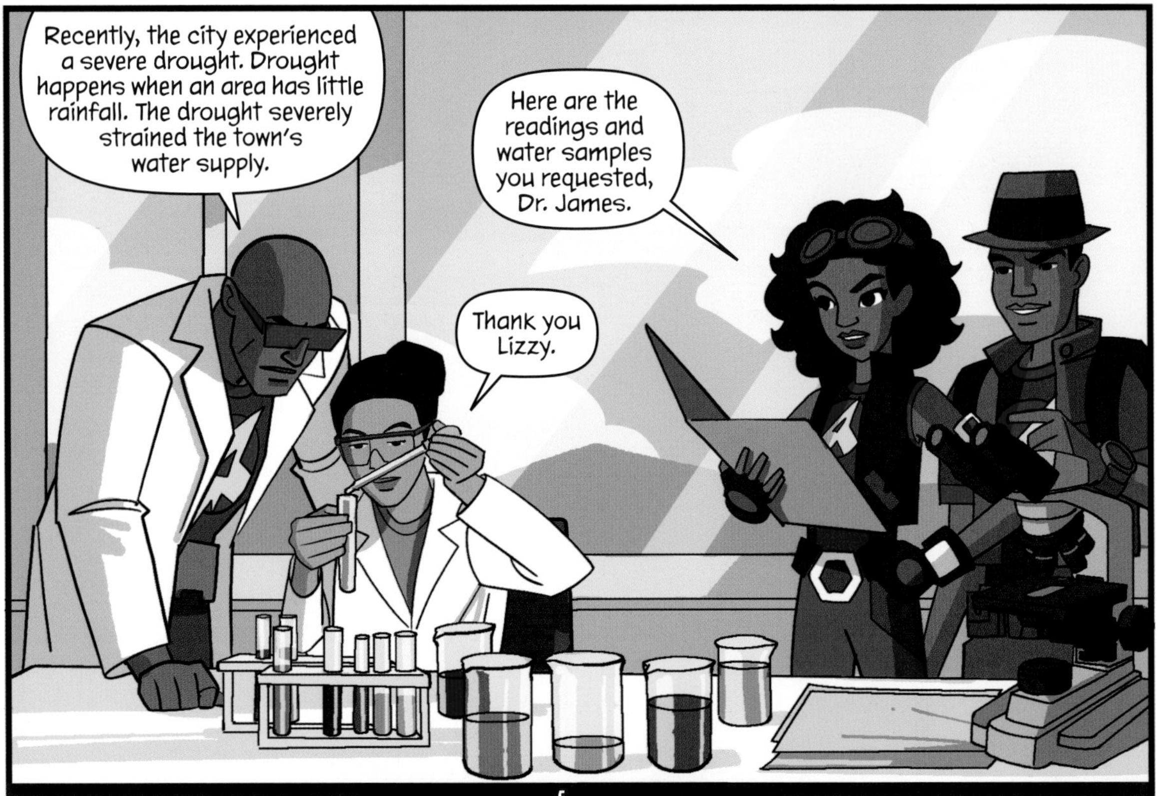
Recently, the city experienced a severe drought. Drought happens when an area has little rainfall. The drought severely strained the town's water supply.
Here are the readings and water samples you requested, Dr. James.
Thank you Lizzy.

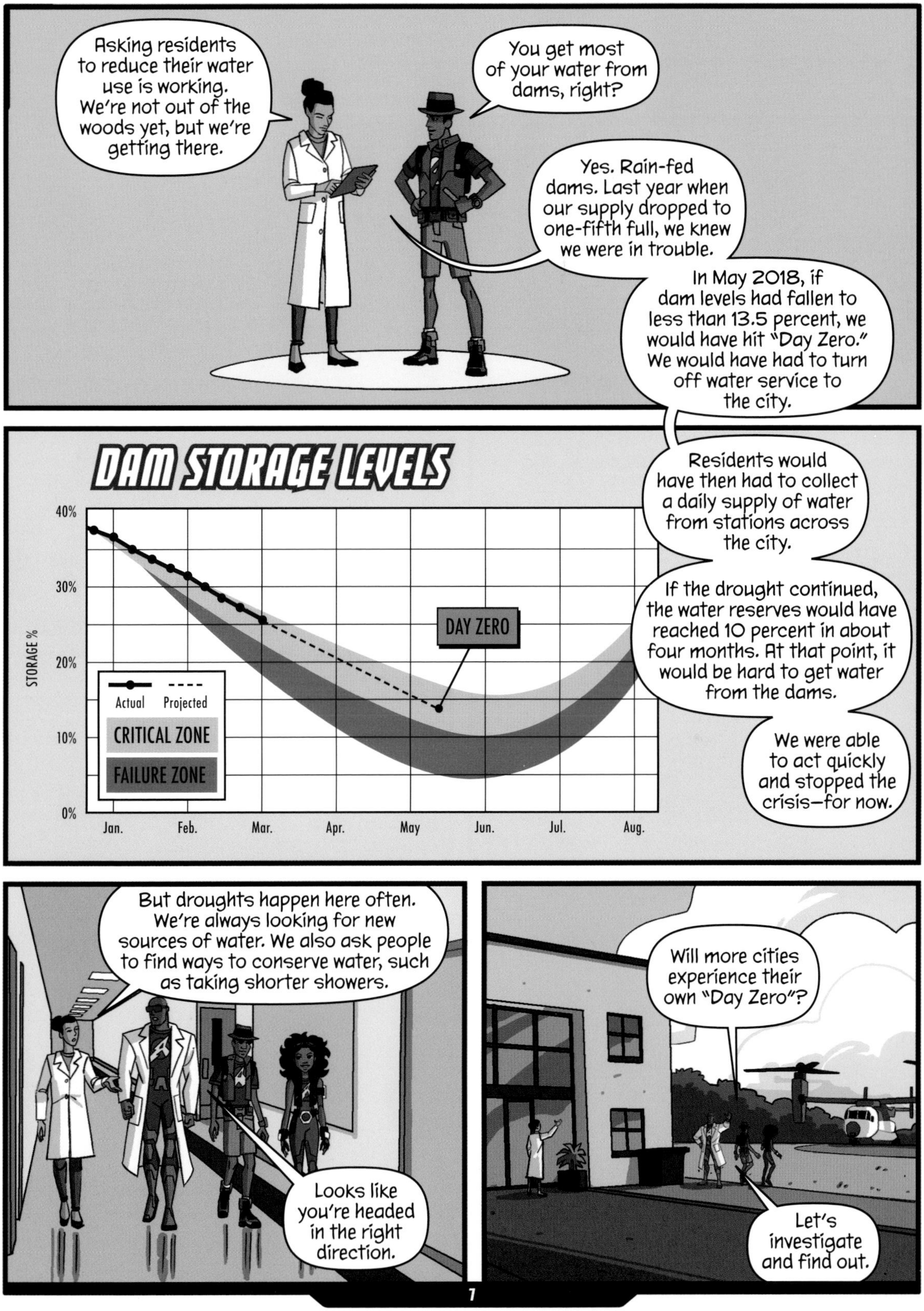

Asking residents to reduce their water use is working. We're not out of the woods yet, but we're getting there.
You get most of your water from dams, right?
Yes. Rain-fed dams. Last year when our supply dropped to one-fifth full, we knew we were in trouble.
In May 2018, if dam levels had fallen to less than 13.5 percent, we would have hit "Day Zero." We would have had to turn off water service to the city.
DAM STORAGE LEVELS
40%
30%
20%
10%
0%
STORAGE %
Jan.
Feb.
Mar.
Apr.
May
Jun.
Jul.
Aug.
DAY ZERO
Actual
Projected
CRITICAL ZONE
FAILURE ZONE
Residents would have then had to collect a daily supply of water from stations across the city.
If the drought continued, the water reserves would have reached 10 percent in about four months. At that point, it would be hard to get water from the dams.
We were able to act quickly and stopped the crisis—for now.
But droughts happen here often. We're always looking for new sources of water. We also ask people to find ways to conserve water, such as taking shorter showers.
Looks like you're headed in the right direction.
Will more cities experience their own "Day Zero"?
Let's investigate and find out.

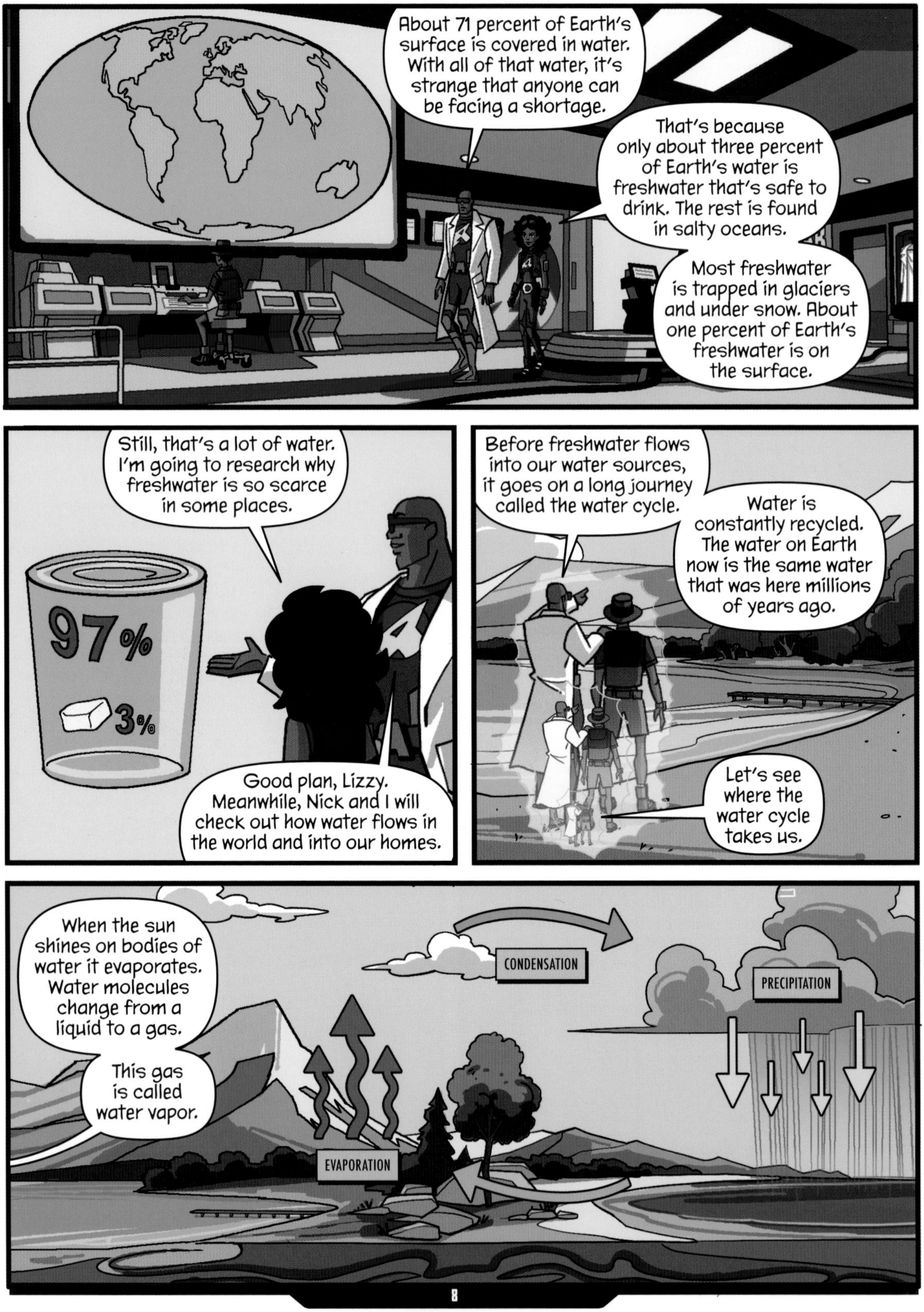
About 71 percent of Earth's surface is covered in water. With all of that water, it's strange that anyone can be facing a shortage.
That's because only about three percent of Earth's water is freshwater that's safe to drink. The rest is found in salty oceans.
Most freshwater is trapped in glaciers and under snow. About one percent of Earth's freshwater is on the surface.
Still, that's a lot of water. I'm going to research why freshwater is so scarce in some places.
97%
3%
Good plan, Lizzy. Meanwhile, Nick and I will check out how water flows in the world and into our homes.
Before freshwater flows into our water sources, it goes on a long journey called the water cycle.
Water is constantly recycled. The water on Earth now is the same water that was here millions of years ago.
Let's see where the water cycle takes us.
When the sun shines on bodies of water it evaporates. Water molecules change from a liquid to a gas.
This gas is called water vapor.
CONDENSATION
PRECIPITATION
EVAPORATION

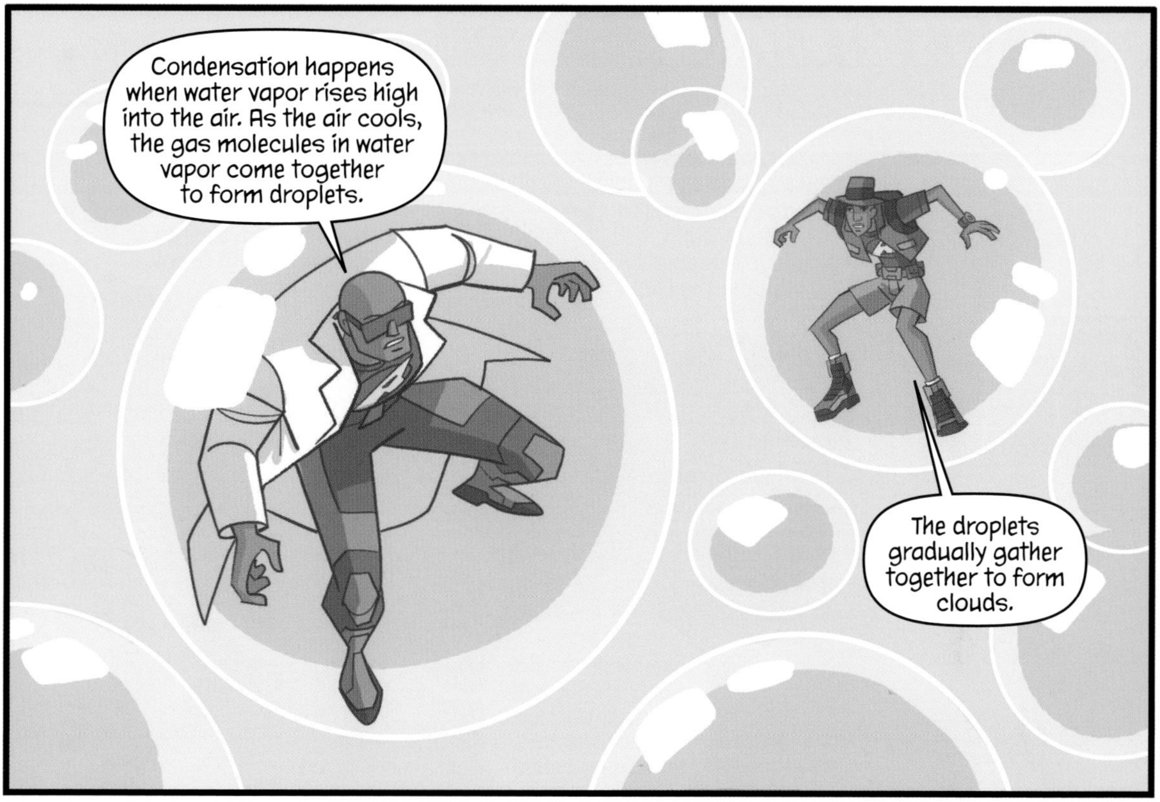
Condensation happens when water vapor rises high into the air. As the air cools, the gas molecules in water vapor come together to form droplets.
The droplets gradually gather together to form clouds.

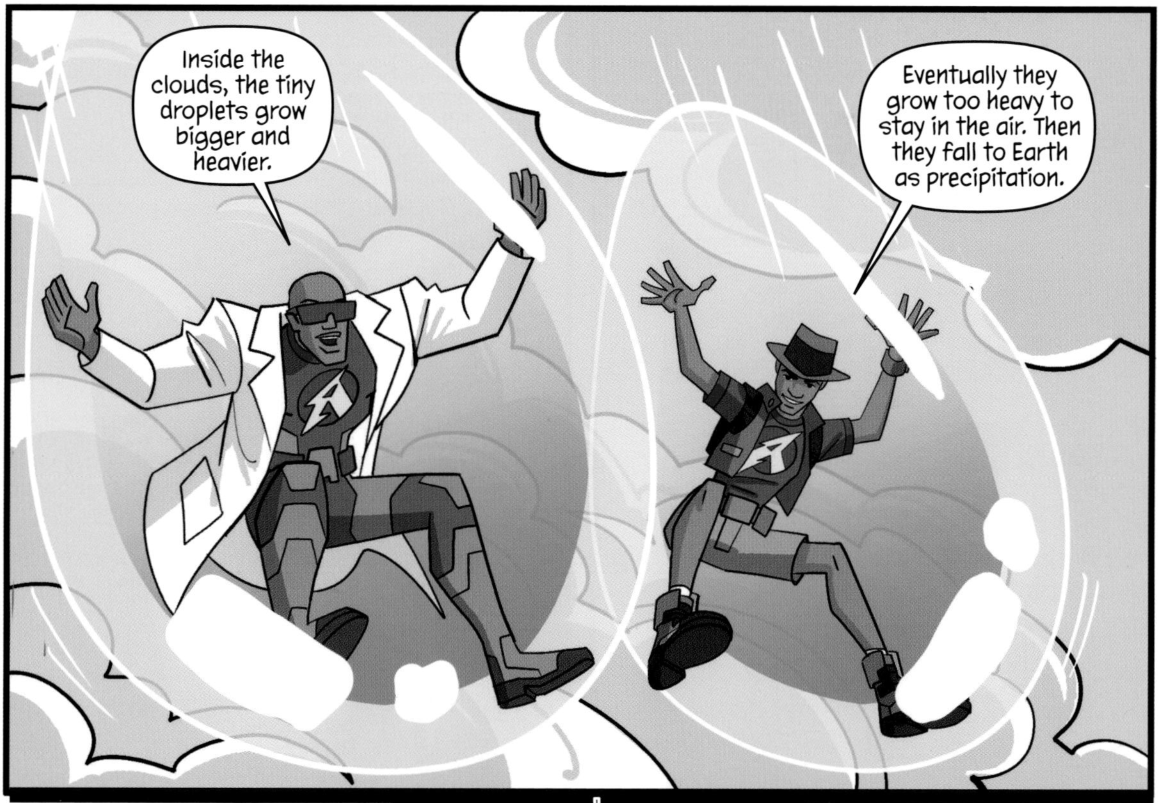
Inside the clouds, the tiny droplets grow bigger and heavier.
Eventually they grow too heavy to stay in the air. Then they fall to Earth as precipitation.

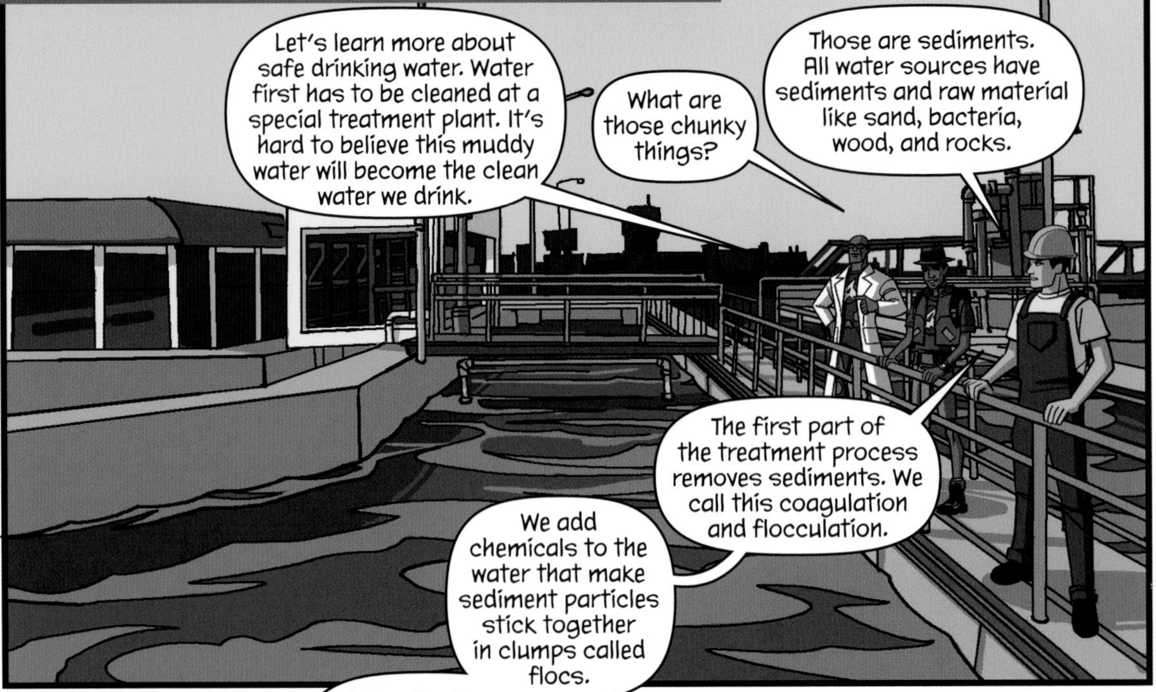
Let's learn more about safe drinking water. Water first has to be cleaned at a special treatment plant. It's hard to believe this muddy water will become the clean water we drink.
What are those chunky things?
Those are sediments. All water sources have sediments and raw material like sand, bacteria, wood, and rocks.
The first part of the treatment process removes sediments. We call this coagulation and flocculation.
We add chemicals to the water that make sediment particles stick together in clumps called flocs.

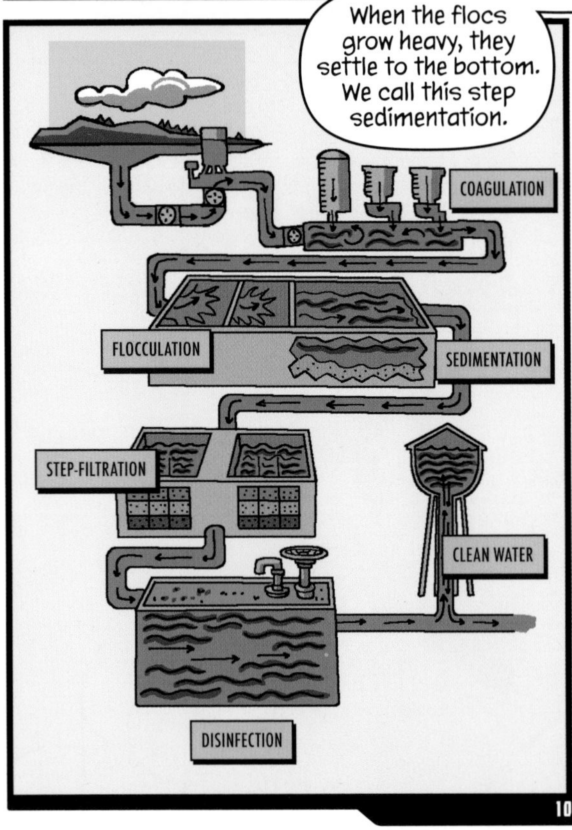
When the flocs grow heavy, they settle to the bottom. We call this step sedimentation.
COAGULATION
FLOCCULATION
SEDIMENTATION
STEP-FILTRATION
CLEAN WATER
DISINFECTION

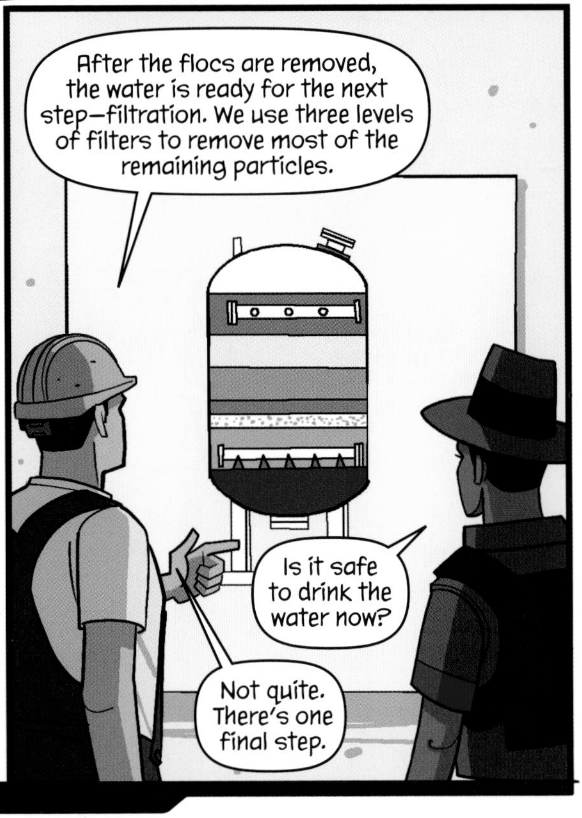
After the flocs are removed, the water is ready for the next step—filtration. We use three levels of filters to remove most of the remaining particles.
Is it safe to drink the water now?
Not quite. There's one final step.

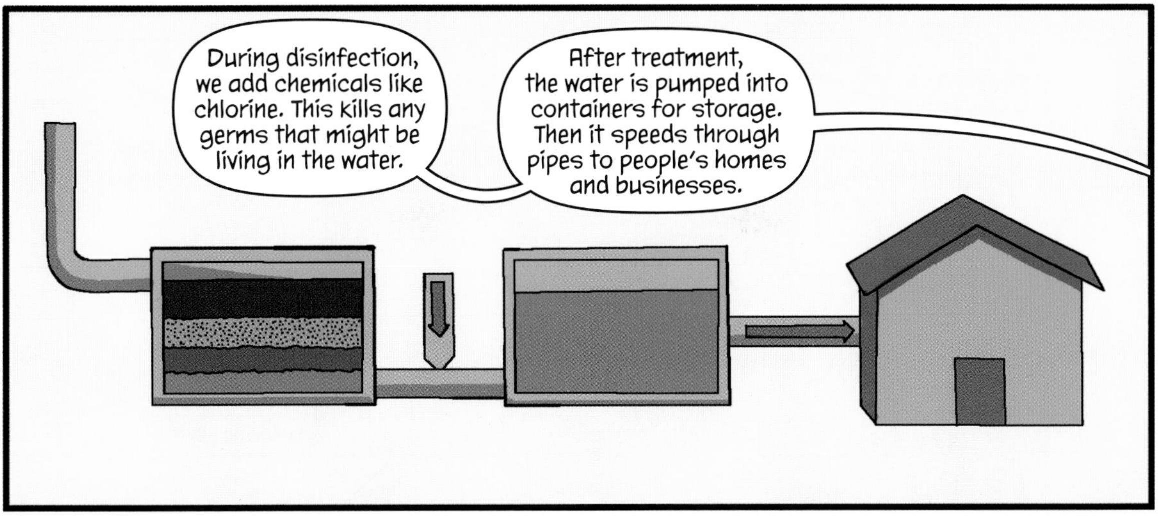
During disinfection, we add chemicals like chlorine. This kills any germs that might be living in the water.
After treatment, the water is pumped into containers for storage. Then it speeds through pipes to people's homes and businesses.

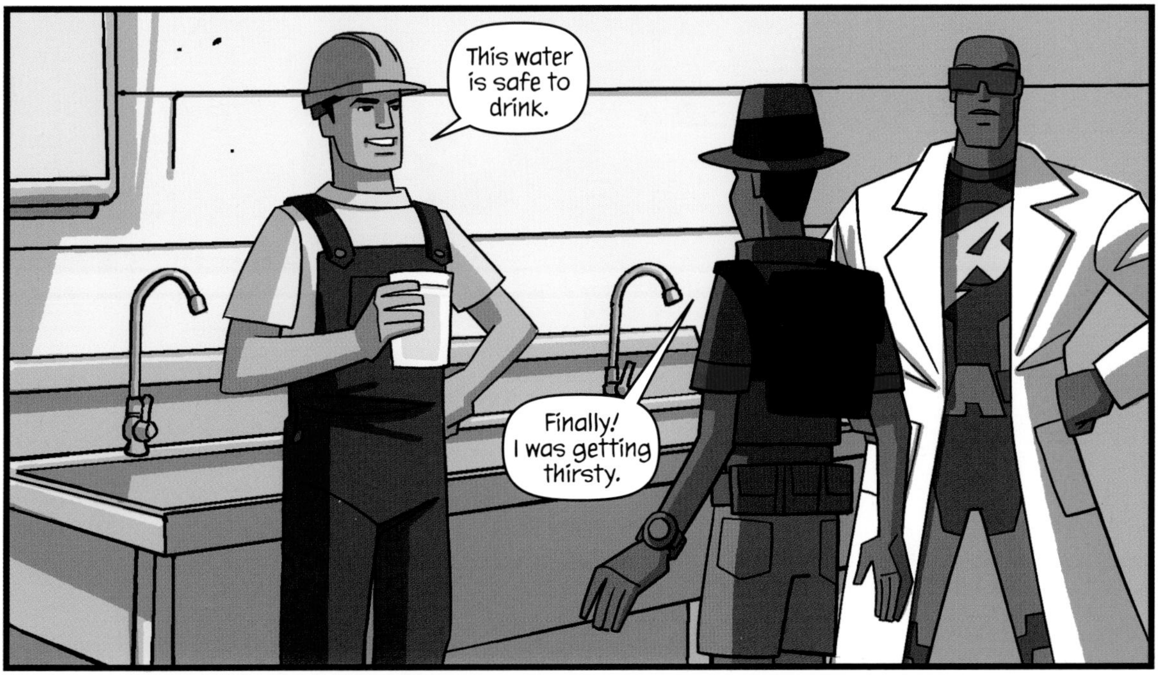
This water is safe to drink.
Finally! I was getting thirsty.

WATER CRISIS IN FLINT, MICHIGAN

Since 2014, the residents of Flint, Michigan, have faced a water crisis. After the city switched its water source to the Flint River, residents noticed the water looked, smelled, and tasted bad. People became ill, and some broke out in rashes. The city hadn't properly treated the water. It was filled with dangerous bacteria and high levels of lead from the city's old pipes. Residents were ordered to use bottled water for everything, including bathing. The city switched back to a safe water source in 2015 and began replacing most of its old pipes. But even though officials later claimed that the water was safe to drink, many residents still refused to use tap water.

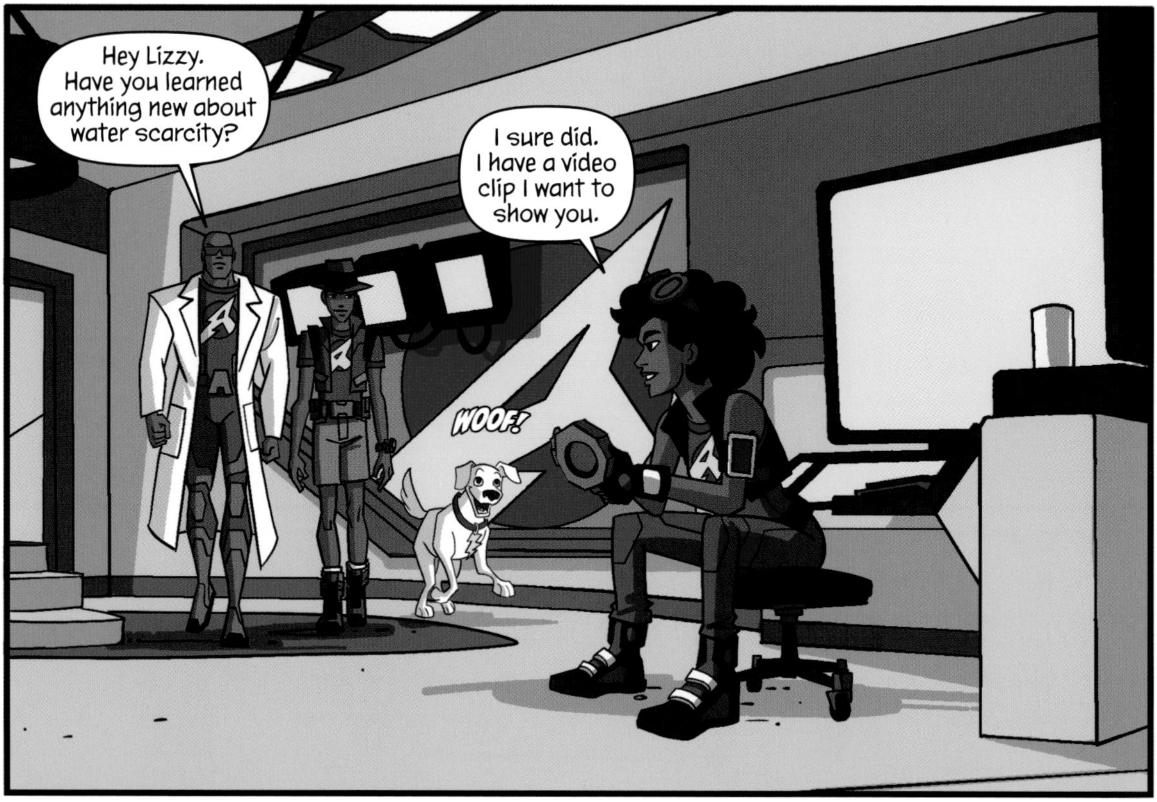
Hey Lizzy. Have you learned anything new about water scarcity?
I sure did. I have a video clip I want to show you.
WOOF!

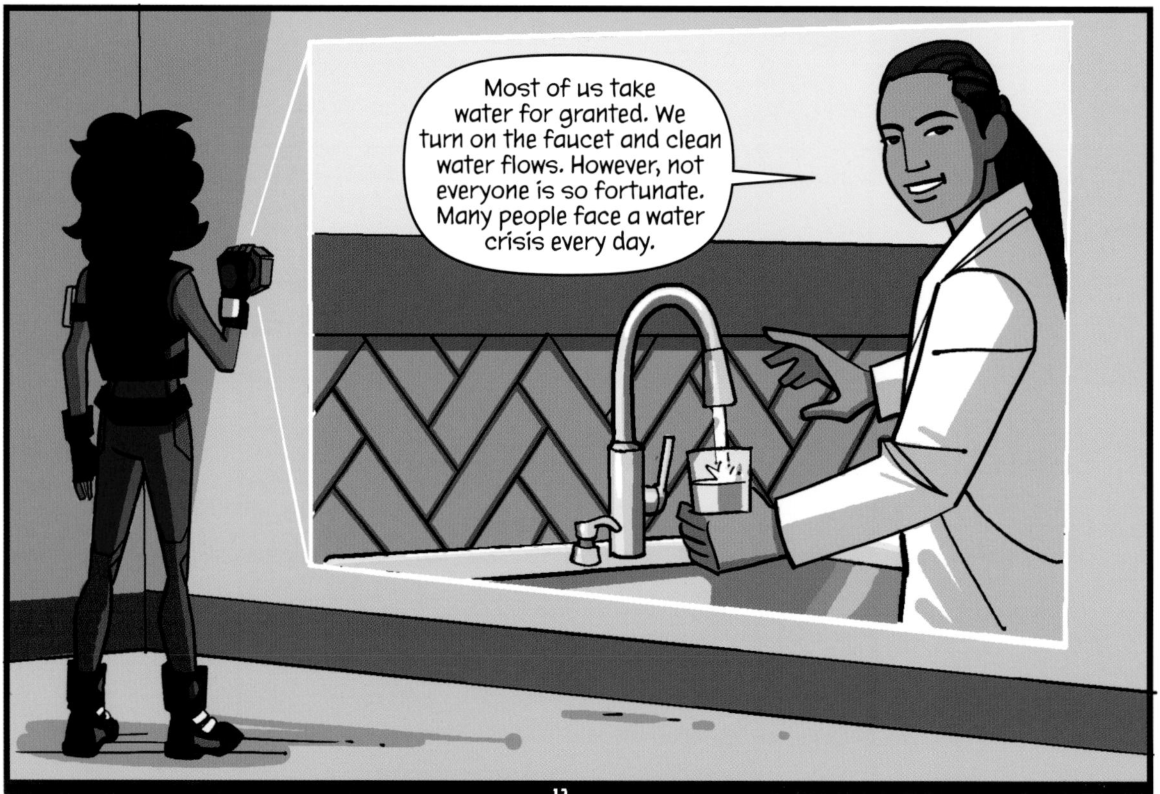
Most of us take water for granted. We turn on the faucet and clean water flows. However, not everyone is so fortunate. Many people face a water crisis every day.

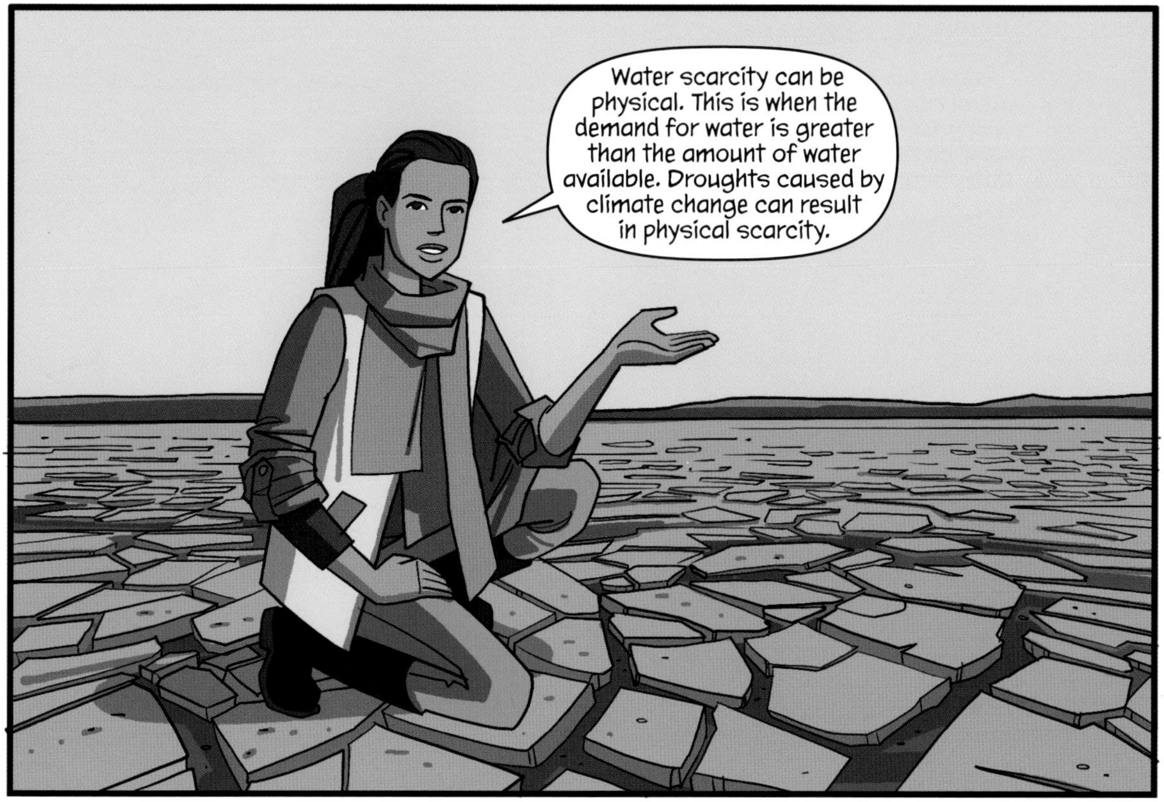
Water scarcity can be physical. This is when the demand for water is greater than the amount of water available. Droughts caused by climate change can result in physical scarcity.

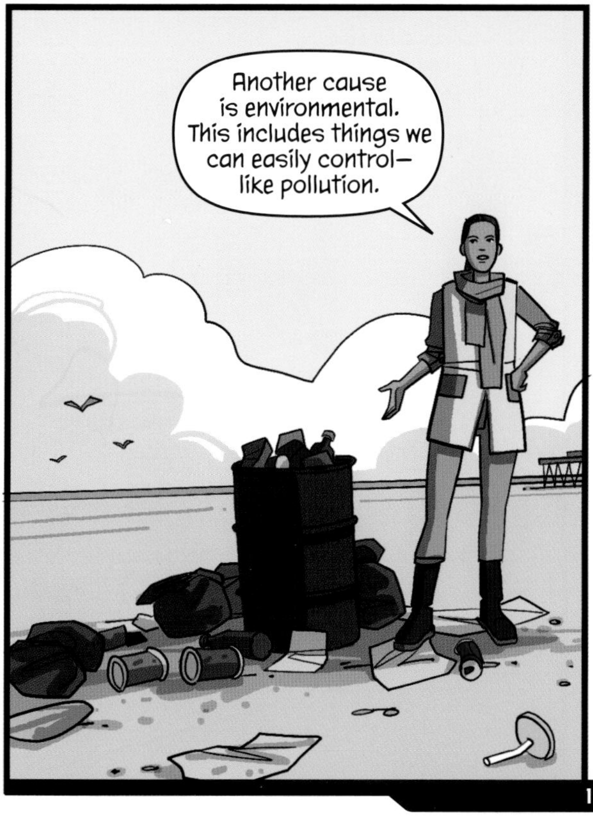
Another cause is environmental. This includes things we can easily control—like pollution.

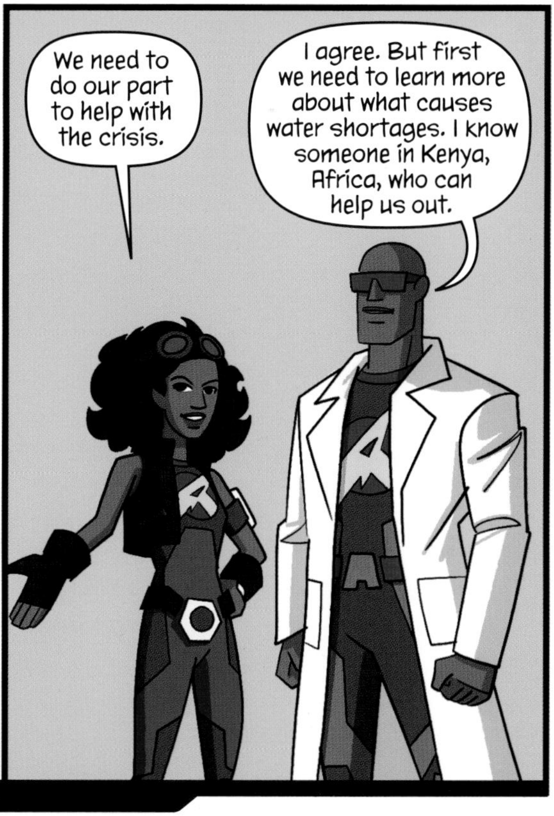
We need to do our part to help with the crisis.
I agree. But first we need to learn more about what causes water shortages. I know someone in Kenya, Africa, who can help us out.

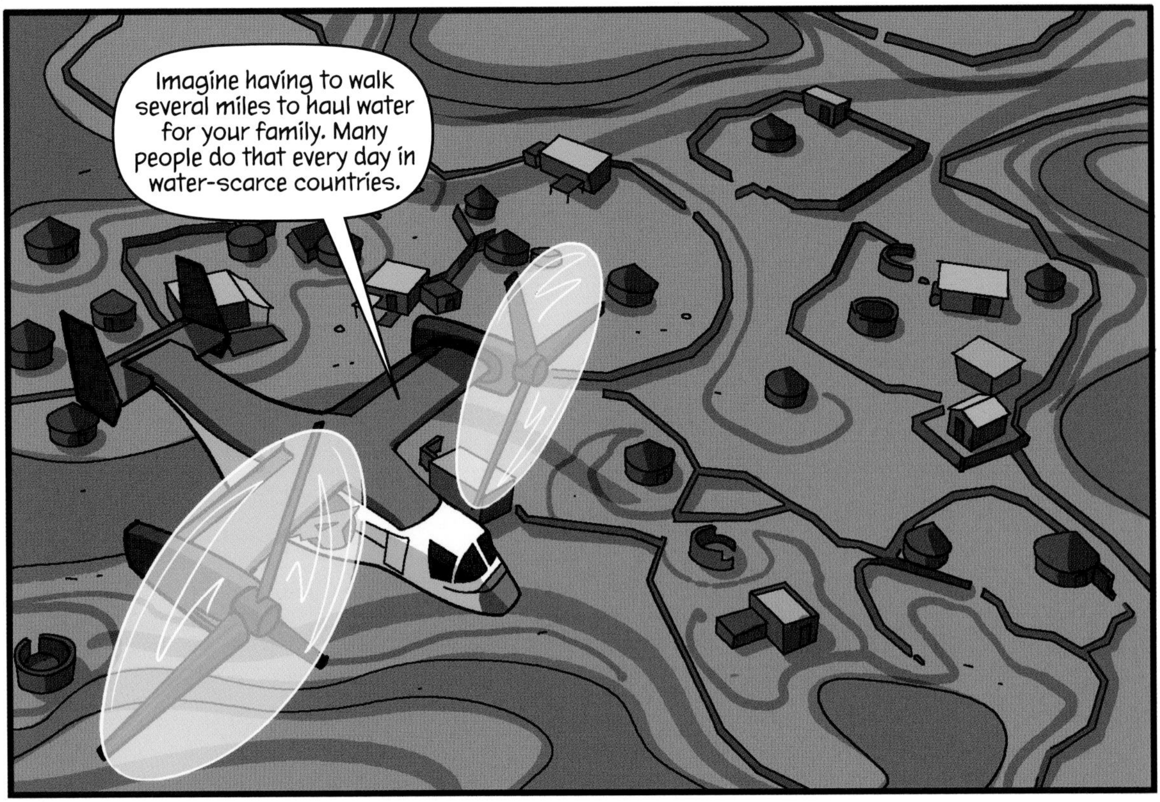
Imagine having to walk several miles to haul water for your family. Many people do that every day in water-scarce countries.

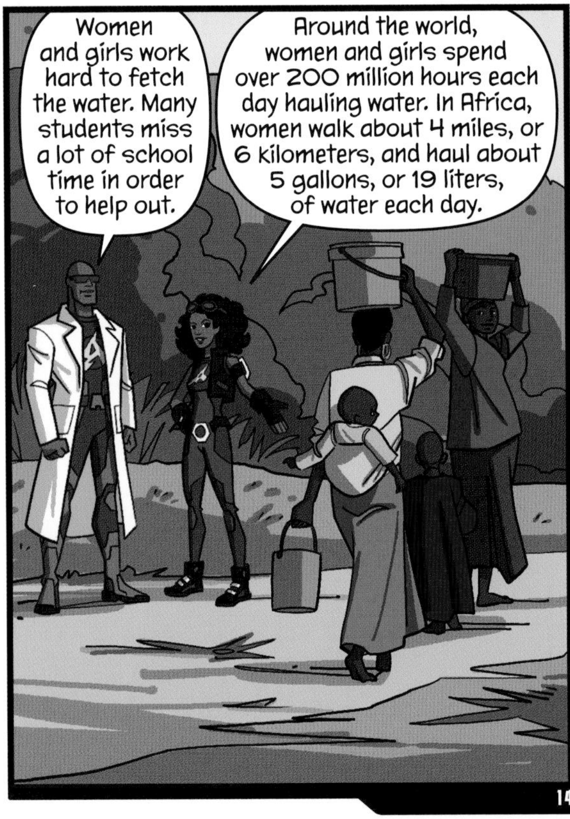
Women and girls work hard to fetch the water. Many students miss a lot of school time in order to help out.
Around the world, women and girls spend over 200 million hours each day hauling water. In Africa, women walk about 4 miles, or 6 kilometers, and haul about 5 gallons, or 19 liters, of water each day.

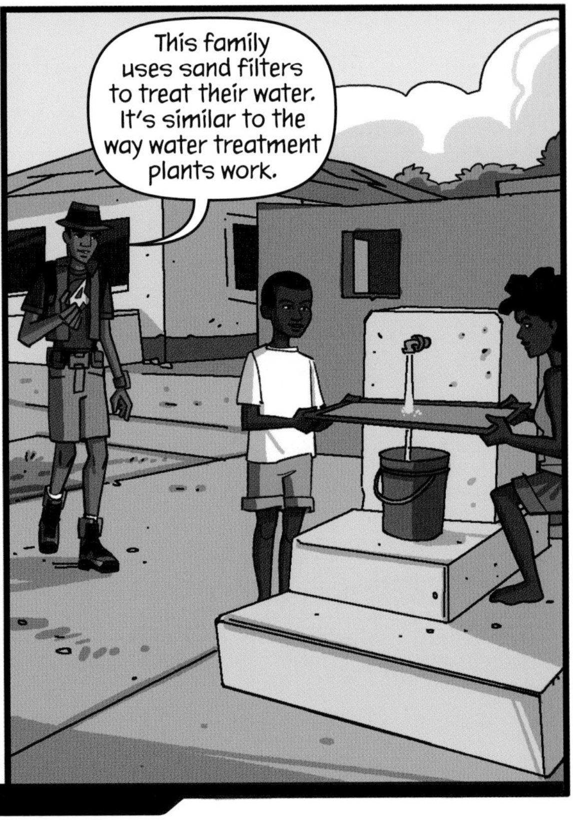
This family uses sand filters to treat their water. It's similar to the way water treatment plants work.

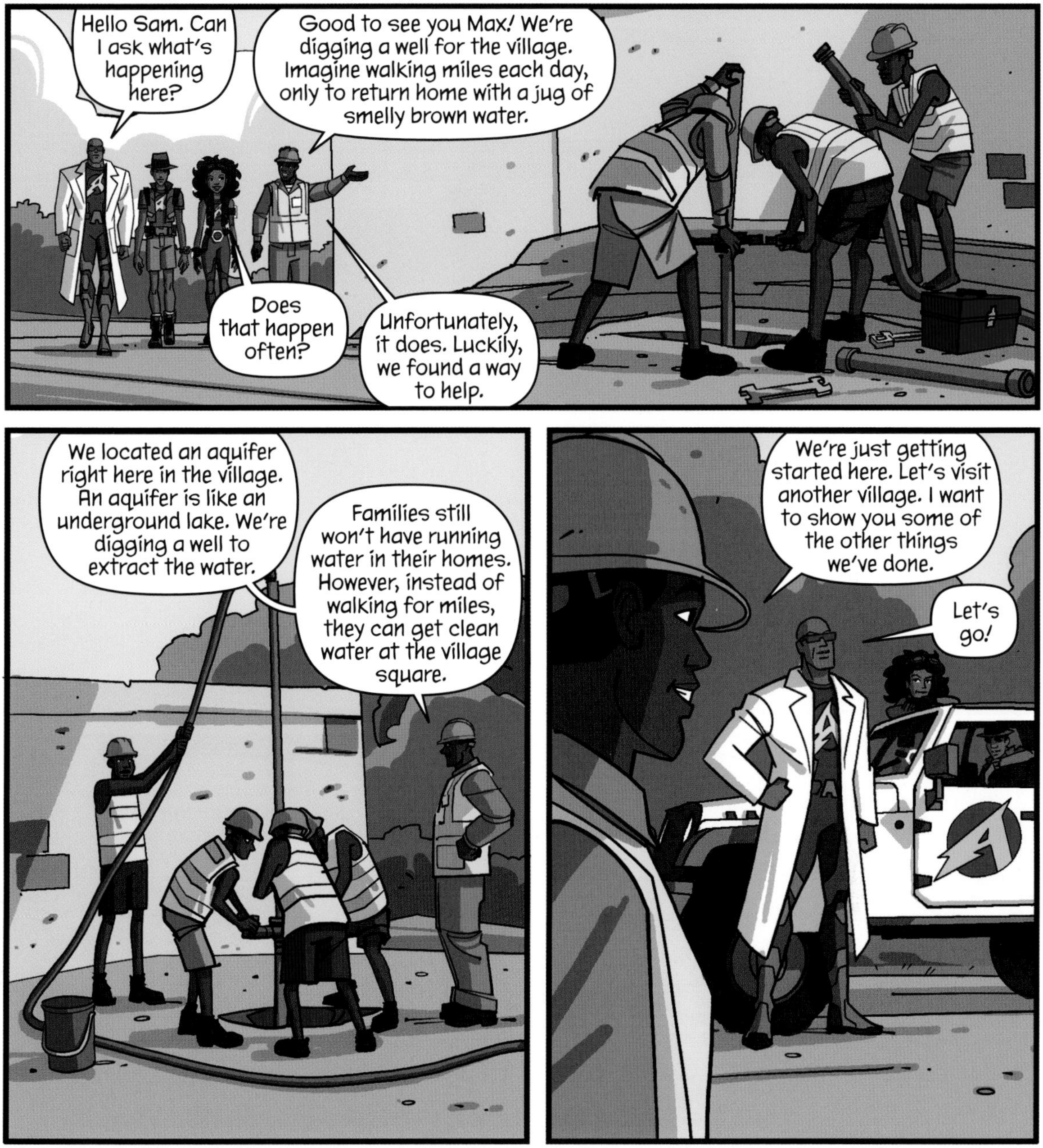
Hello Sam. Can I ask what's happening here?
Good to see you Max! We're digging a well for the village. Imagine walking miles each day, only to return home with a jug of smelly brown water.
Does that happen often?
Unfortunately, it does. Luckily, we found a way to help.
We located an aquifer right here in the village. An aquifer is like an underground lake. We're digging a well to extract the water.
Families still won't have running water in their homes. However, instead of walking for miles, they can get clean water at the village square.
We're just getting started here. Let's visit another village. I want to show you some of the other things we've done.
Let's go!

WHAT IS YOUR WATER FOOTPRINT?

A water footprint includes the amount of water a person uses directly, such as when we take a shower or clean dishes. But our water footprint also includes water we don't see, such as water used to produce goods and services. For example, it takes more than 2,100 gallons of water to produce just one pair of jeans. Knowing our water footprint helps us learn ways to decrease unnecessary water usage.

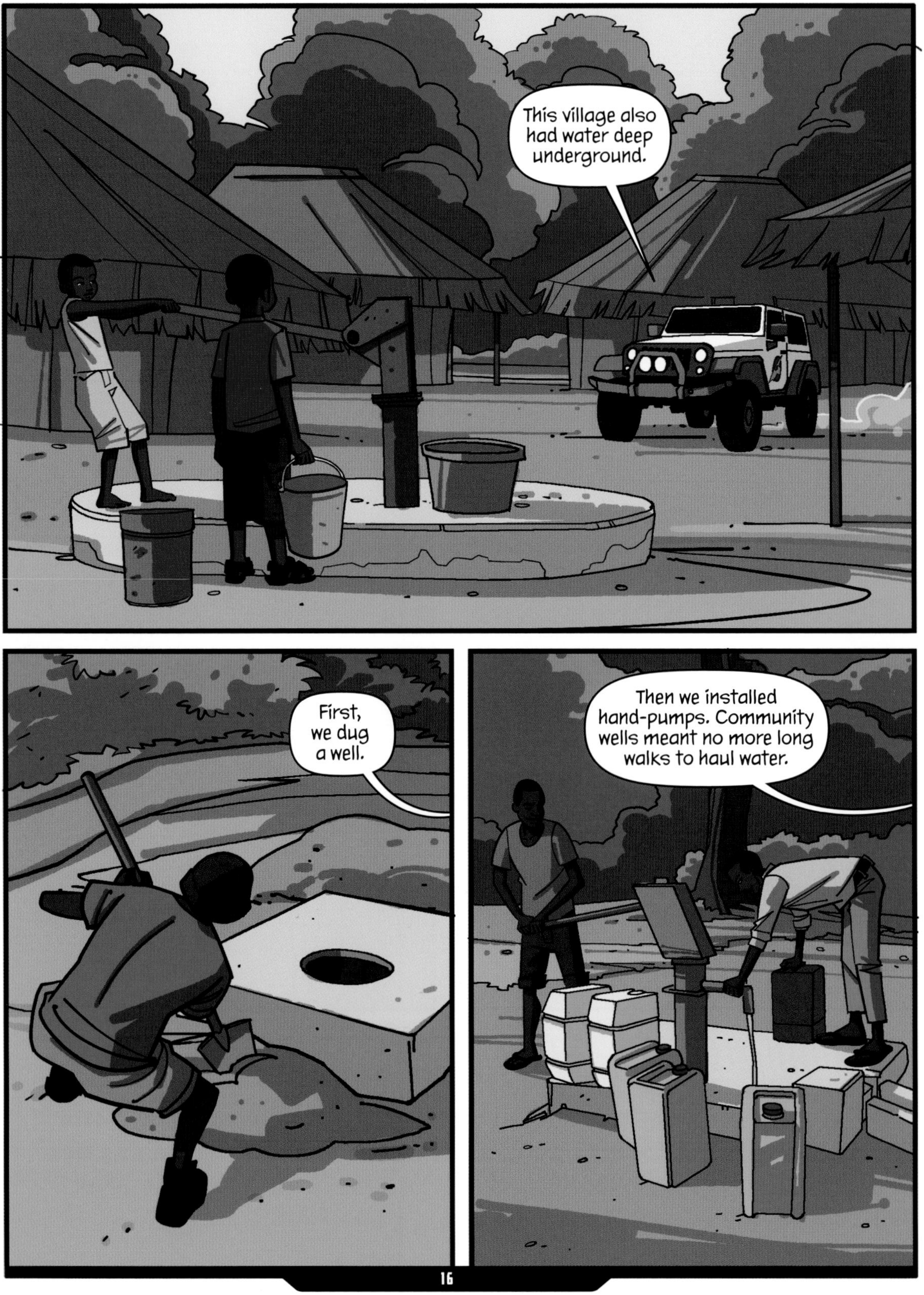
This village also had water deep underground.
First, we dug a well.
Then we installed hand-pumps. Community wells meant no more long walks to haul water.

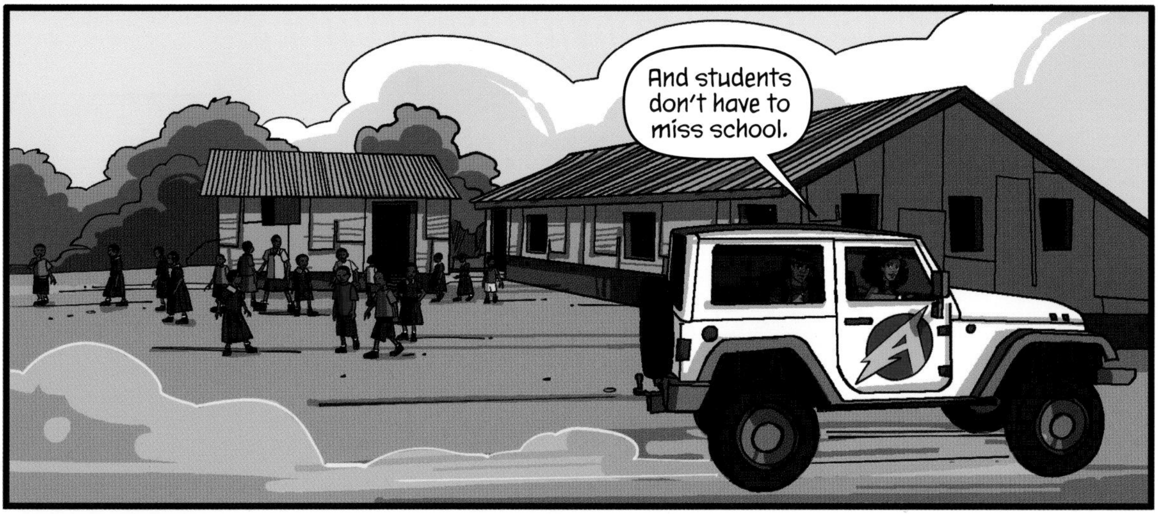
And students don't have to miss school.

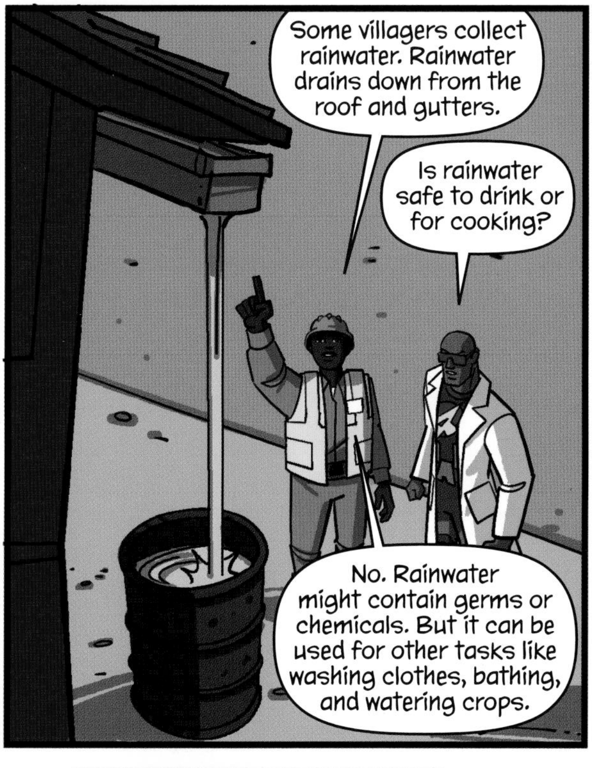
Some villagers collect rainwater. Rainwater drains down from the roof and gutters.
Is rainwater safe to drink or for cooking?
No. Rainwater might contain germs or chemicals. But it can be used for other tasks like washing clothes, bathing, and watering crops.

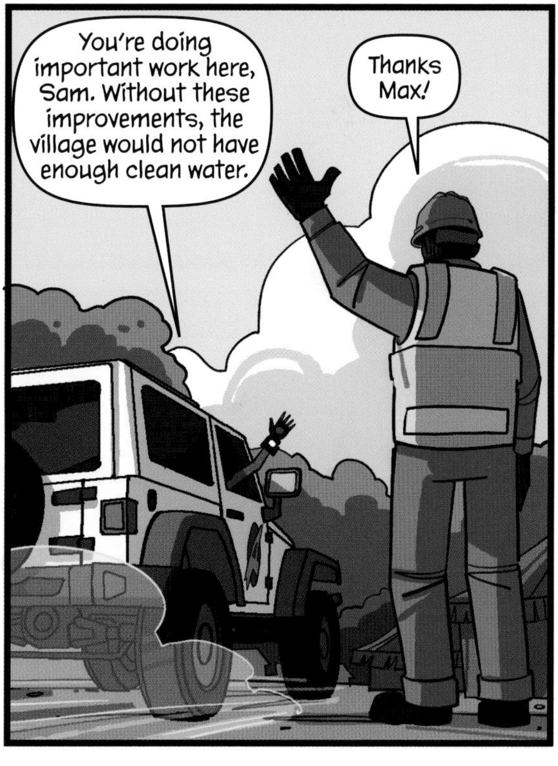
You're doing important work here, Sam. Without these improvements, the village would not have enough clean water.
Thanks Max!

THE CYCLOCLEAN

A Japanese company has come up with a way to clean dirty water and get a workout! The Cycloclean is a bike-powered filtration system. Users ride the bike to the water source. After lowering a hose into the water, they climb on their bike and pedal. Water is pumped through filters, then released into a container. The rider then pedals home with clean water.

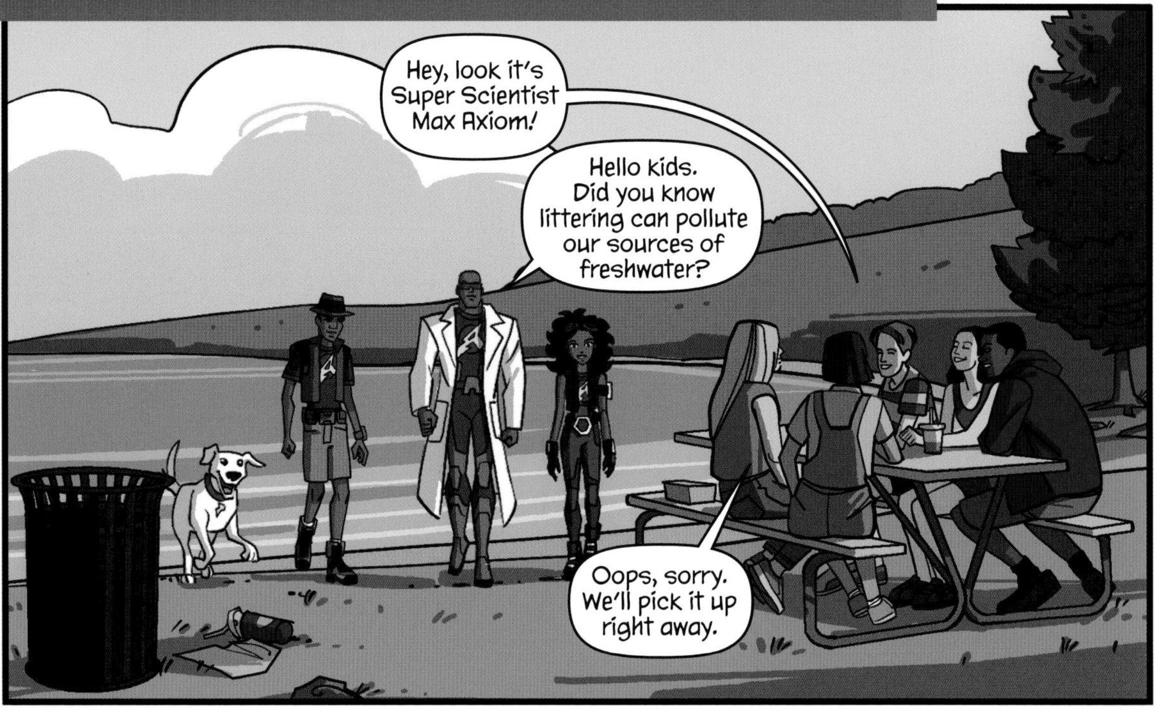
Hey, look it's Super Scientist Max Axiom!
Hello kids. Did you know littering can pollute our sources of freshwater?
Oops, sorry. We'll pick it up right away.

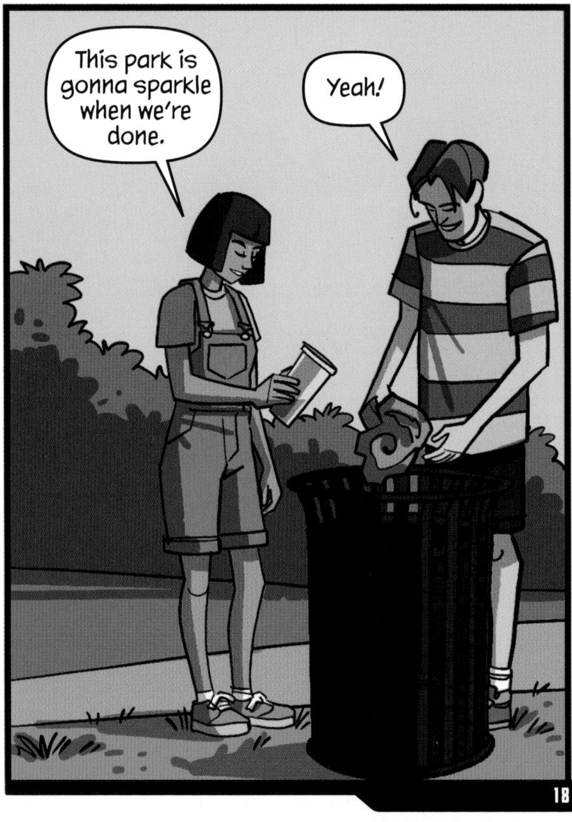
This park is gonna sparkle when we're done.
Yeah!

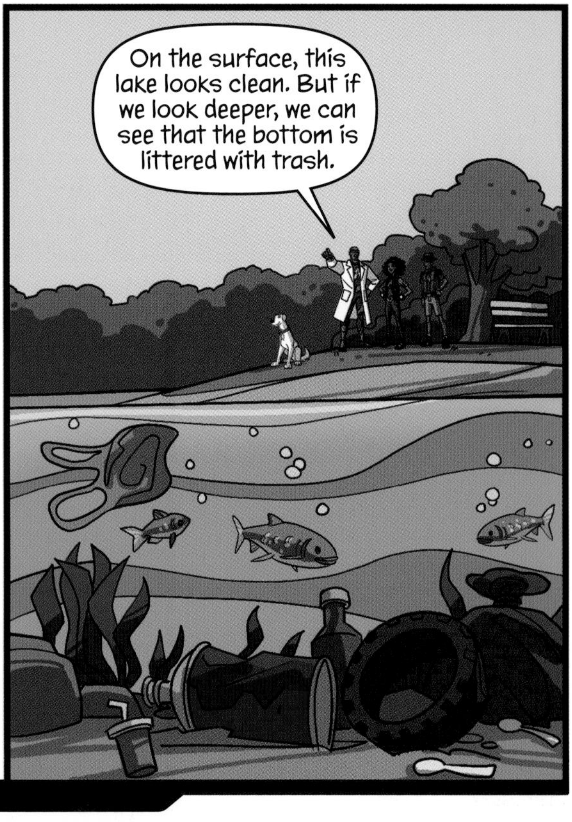
On the surface, this lake looks clean. But if we look deeper, we can see that the bottom is littered with trash.

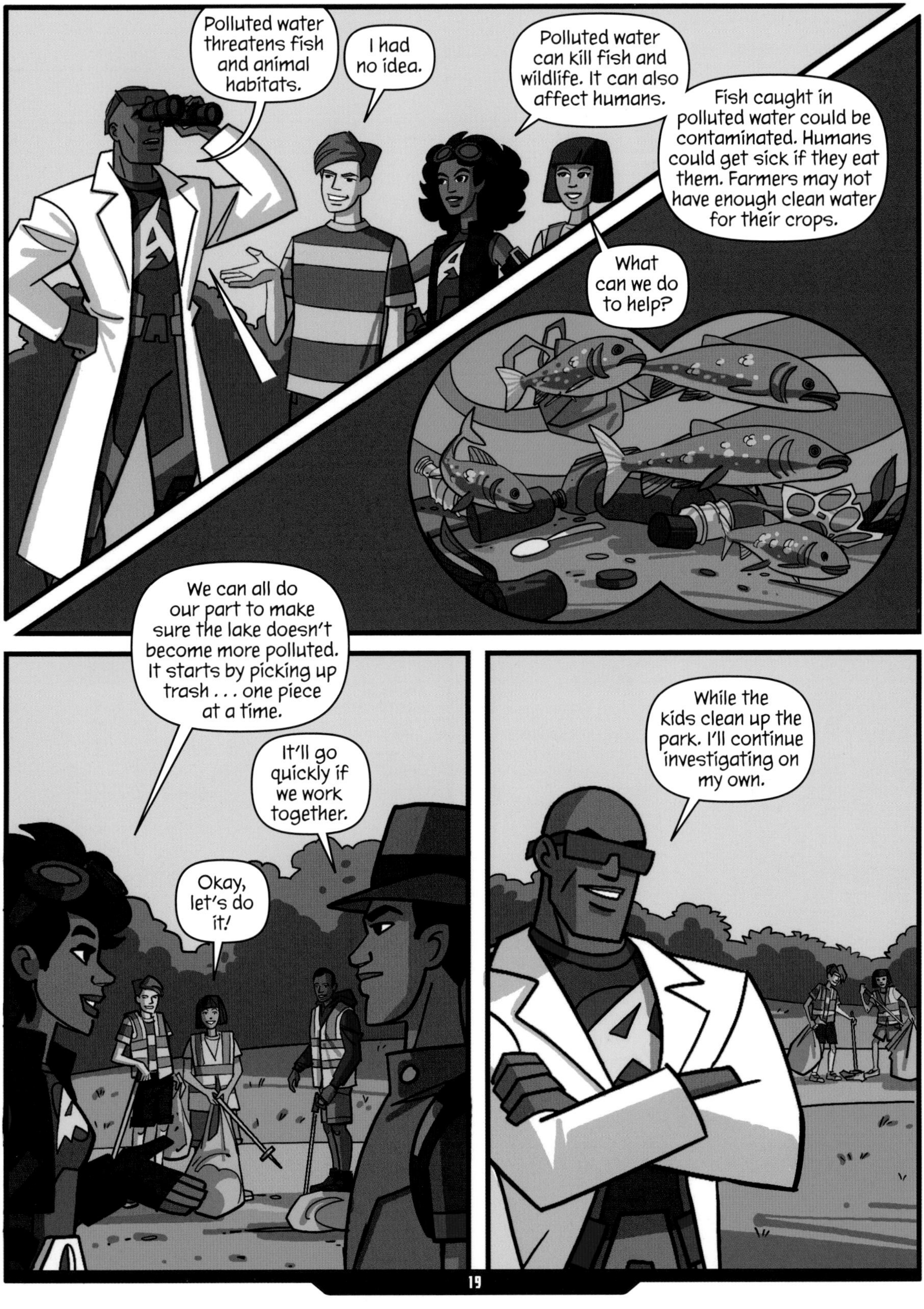
Polluted water threatens fish and animal habitats.
I had no idea.
Polluted water can kill fish and wildlife. It can also affect humans.
Fish caught in polluted water could be contaminated. Humans could get sick if they eat them. Farmers may not have enough clean water for their crops.
What can we do to help?
We can all do our part to make sure the lake doesn't become more polluted. It starts by picking up trash . . . one piece at a time.
It'll go quickly if we work together.
Okay, let's do it!
While the kids clean up the park. I'll continue investigating on my own.

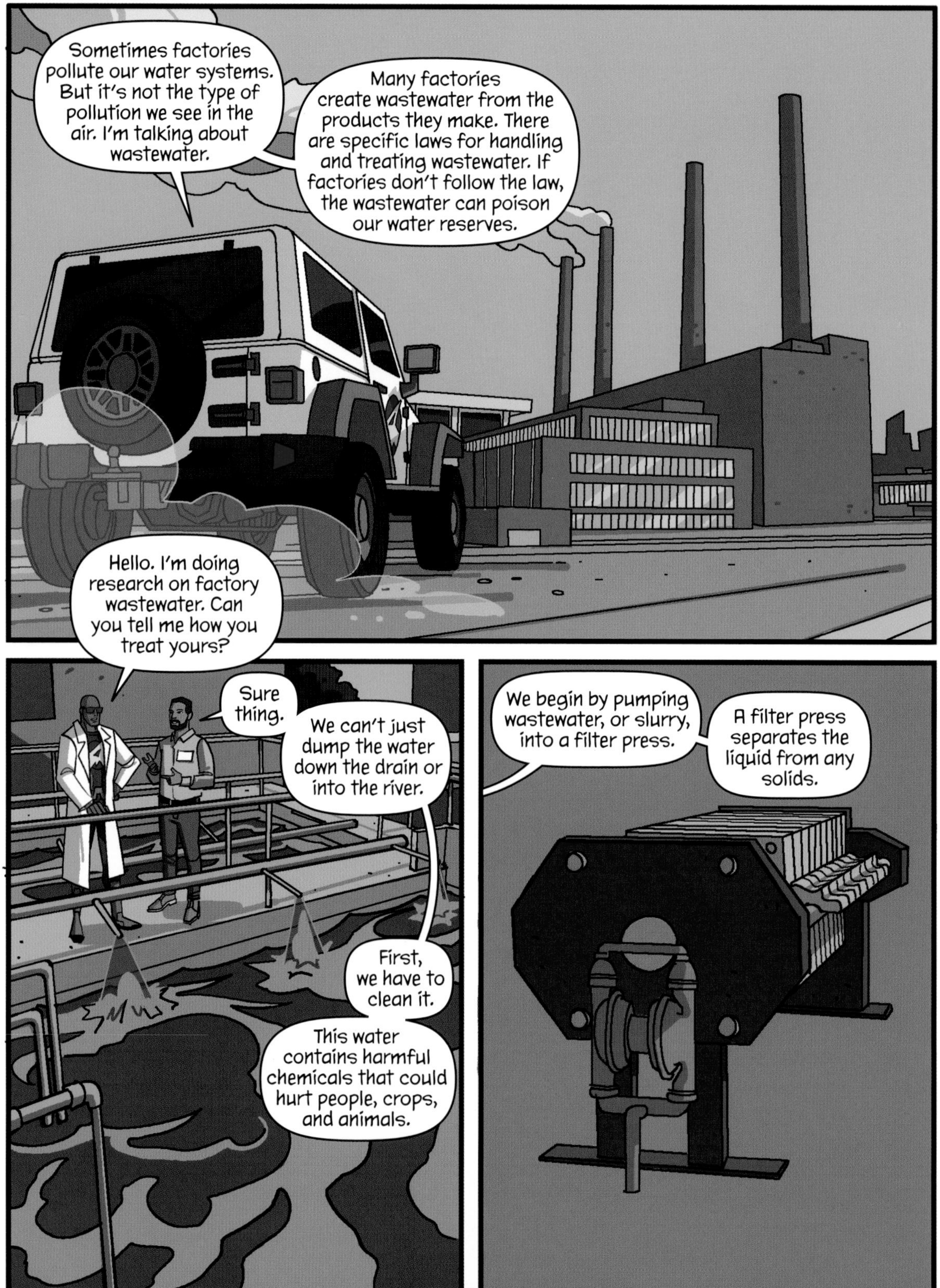
Sometimes factories pollute our water systems. But it's not the type of pollution we see in the air. I'm talking about wastewater.
Many factories create wastewater from the products they make. There are specific laws for handling and treating wastewater. If factories don't follow the law, the wastewater can poison our water reserves.
Hello. I'm doing research on factory wastewater. Can you tell me how you treat yours?
Sure thing.
We can't just dump the water down the drain or into the river.
First, we have to clean it.
This water contains harmful chemicals that could hurt people, crops, and animals.
We begin by pumping wastewater, or slurry, into a filter press.
A filter press separates the liquid from any solids.

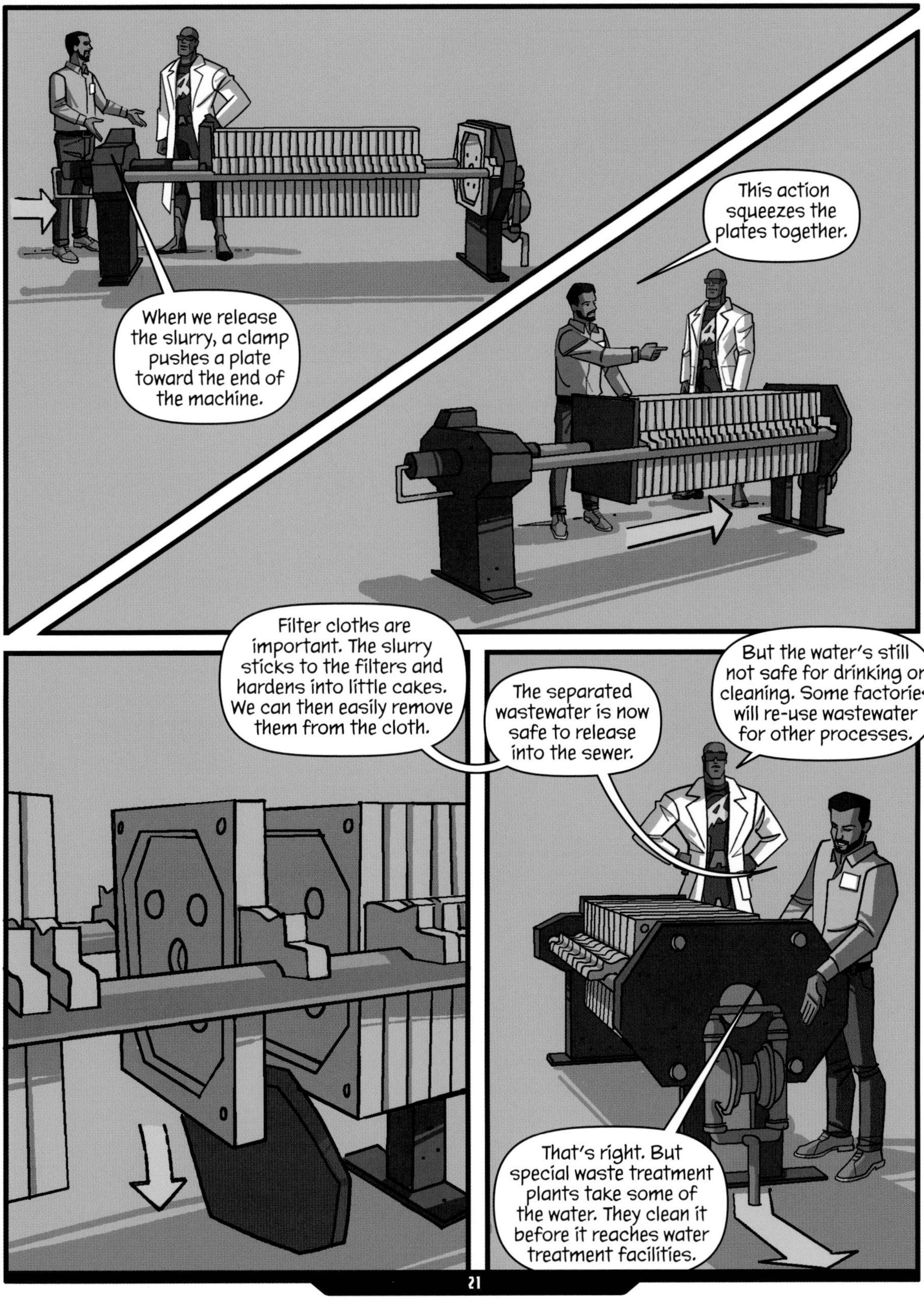
When we release the slurry, a clamp pushes a plate toward the end of the machine.
This action squeezes the plates together.
Filter cloths are important. The slurry sticks to the filters and hardens into little cakes. We can then easily remove them from the cloth.
The separated wastewater is now safe to release into the sewer.
But the water's still not safe for drinking or cleaning. Some factories will re-use wastewater for other processes.
That's right. But special waste treatment plants take some of the water. They clean it before it reaches water treatment facilities.

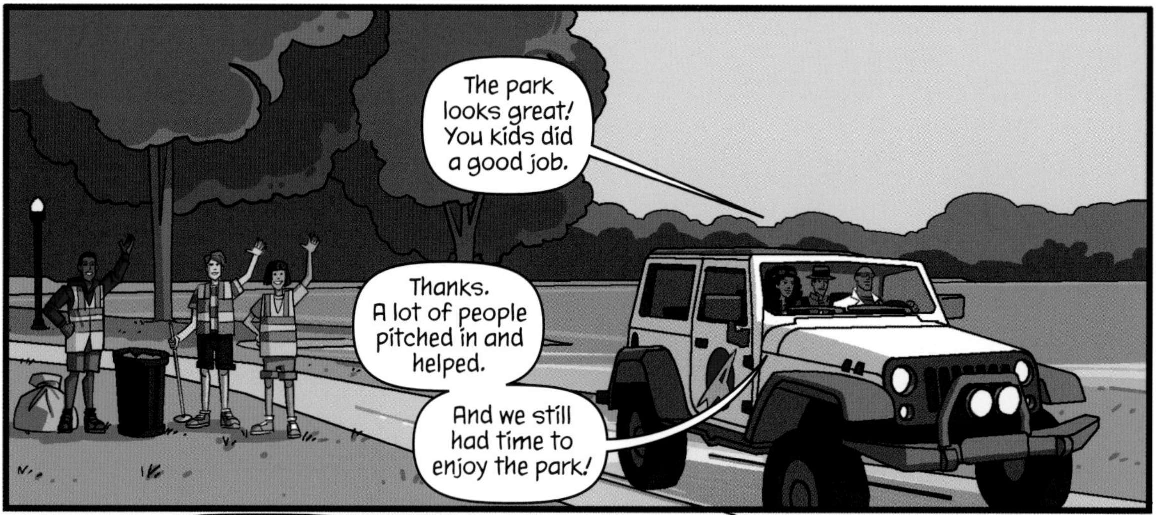
The park looks great! You kids did a good job.
Thanks. A lot of people pitched in and helped.
And we still had time to enjoy the park!

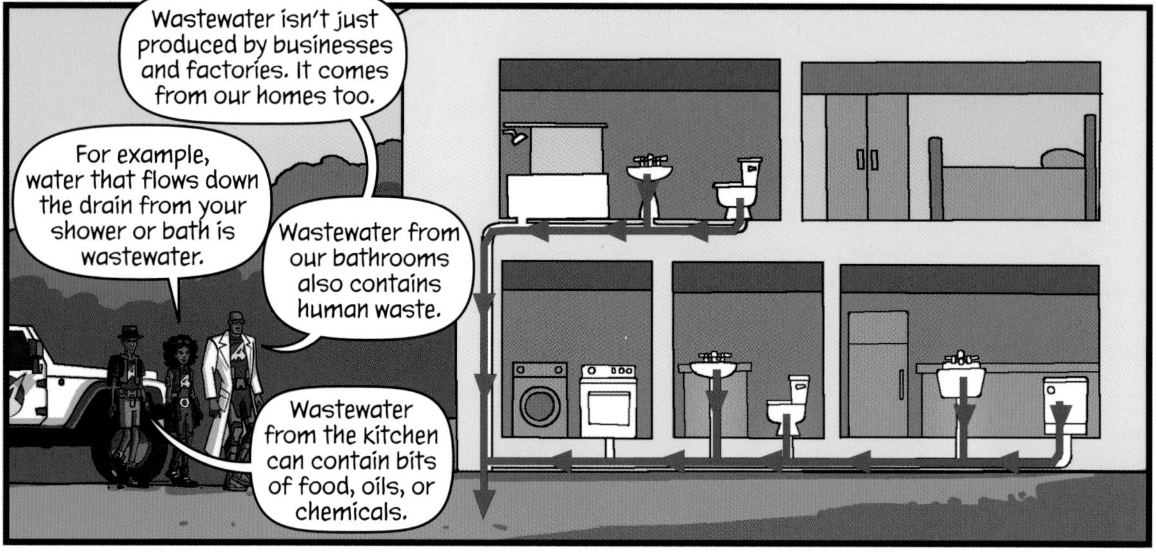
Wastewater isn't just produced by businesses and factories. It comes from our homes too.
For example, water that flows down the drain from your shower or bath is wastewater.
Wastewater from our bathrooms also contains human waste.
Wastewater from the kitchen can contain bits of food, oils, or chemicals.

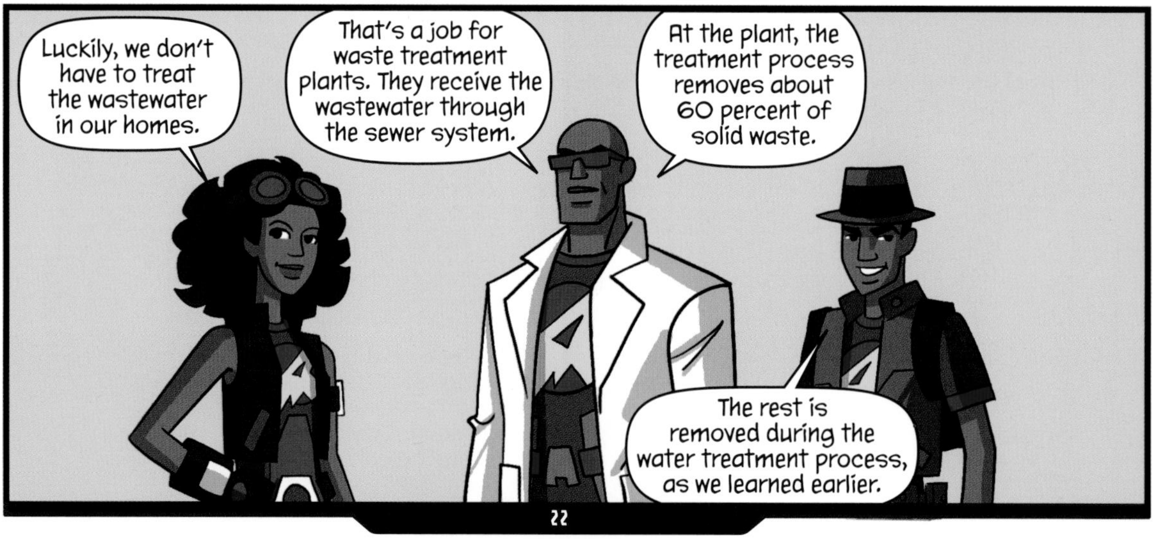
Luckily, we don't have to treat the wastewater in our homes.
That's a job for waste treatment plants. They receive the wastewater through the sewer system.
At the plant, the treatment process removes about 60 percent of solid waste.
The rest is removed during the water treatment process, as we learned earlier.

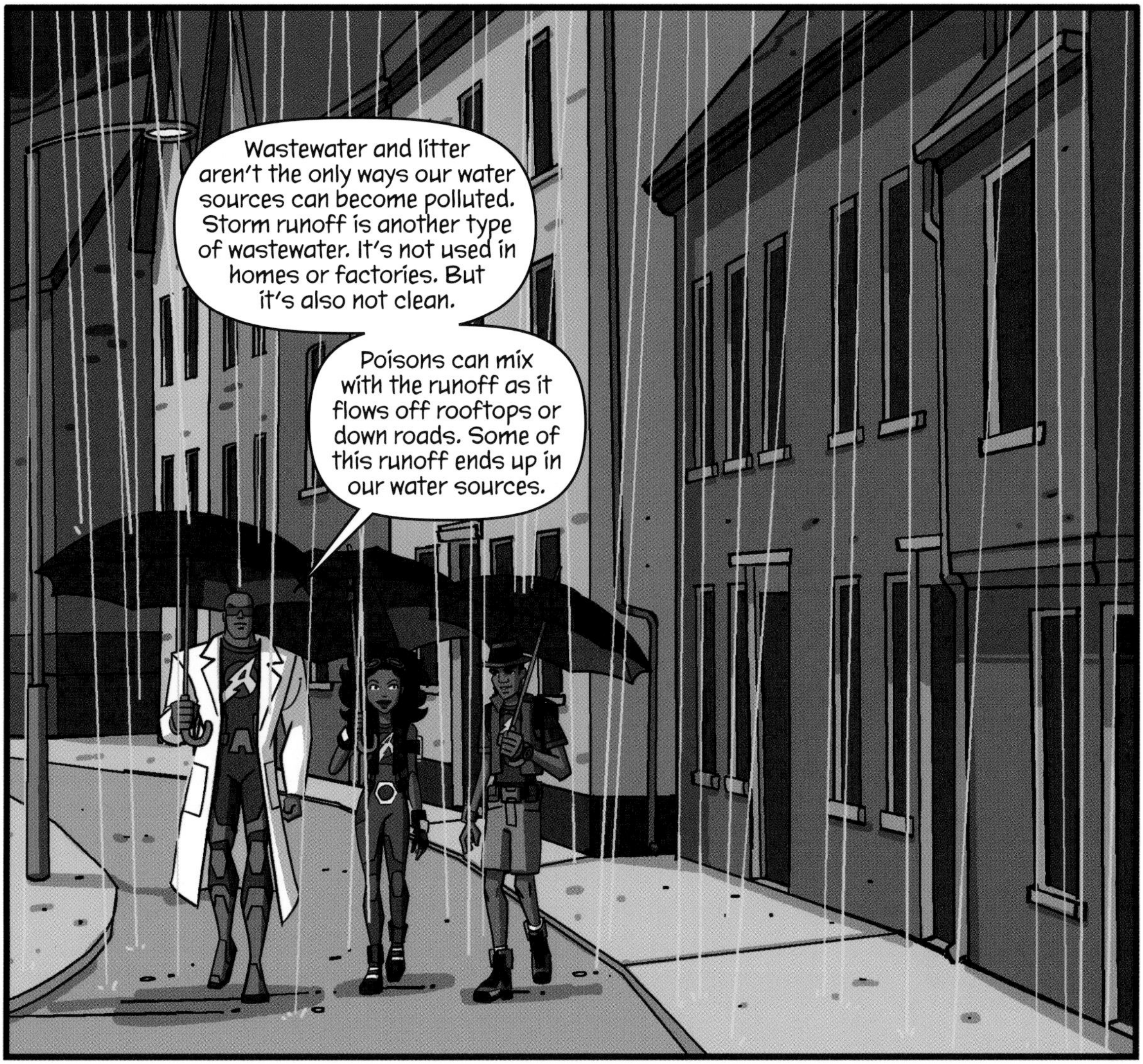
Wastewater and litter aren't the only ways our water sources can become polluted. Storm runoff is another type of wastewater. It's not used in homes or factories. But it's also not clean.
Poisons can mix with the runoff as it flows off rooftops or down roads. Some of this runoff ends up in our water sources.

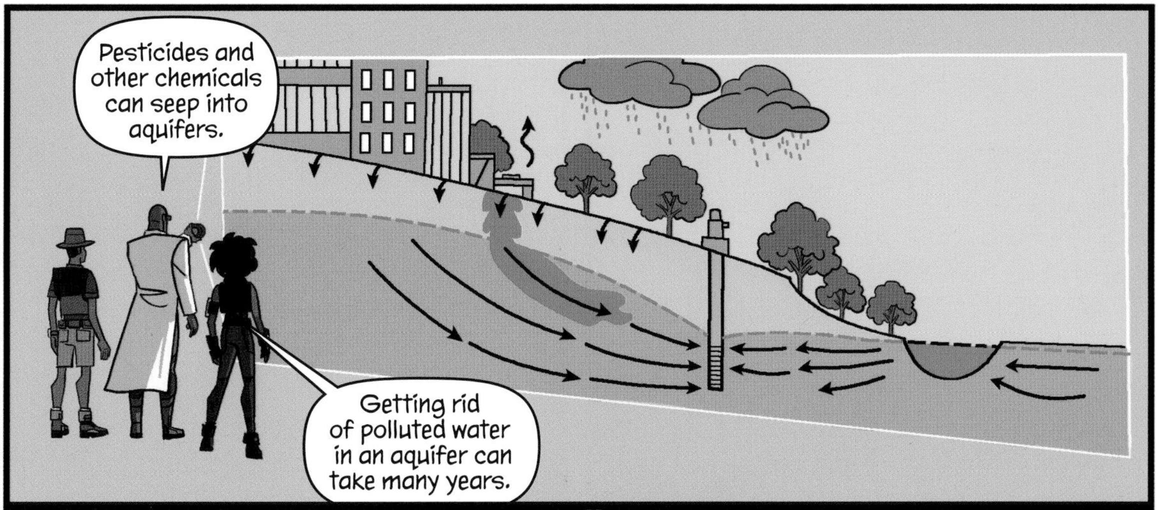
Pesticides and other chemicals can seep into aquifers.
Getting rid of polluted water in an aquifer can take many years.

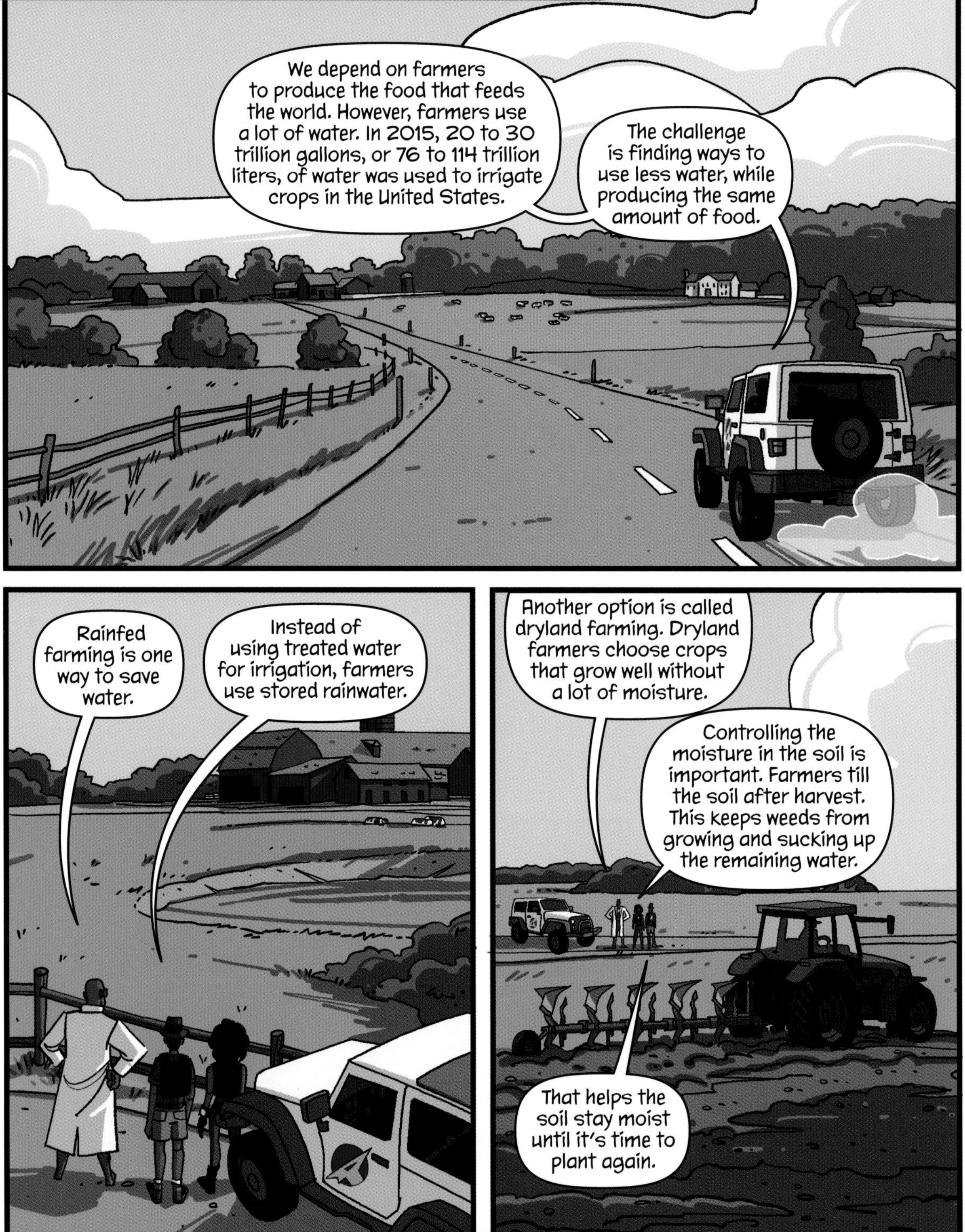
We depend on farmers to produce the food that feeds the world. However, farmers use a lot of water. In 2015, 20 to 30 trillion gallons, or 76 to 114 trillion liters, of water was used to irrigate crops in the United States.
The challenge is finding ways to use less water, while producing the same amount of food.
Rainfed farming is one way to save water.
Instead of using treated water for irrigation, farmers use stored rainwater.
Another option is called dryland farming. Dryland farmers choose crops that grow well without a lot of moisture.
Controlling the moisture in the soil is important. Farmers till the soil after harvest. This keeps weeds from growing and sucking up the remaining water.
That helps the soil stay moist until it's time to plant again.

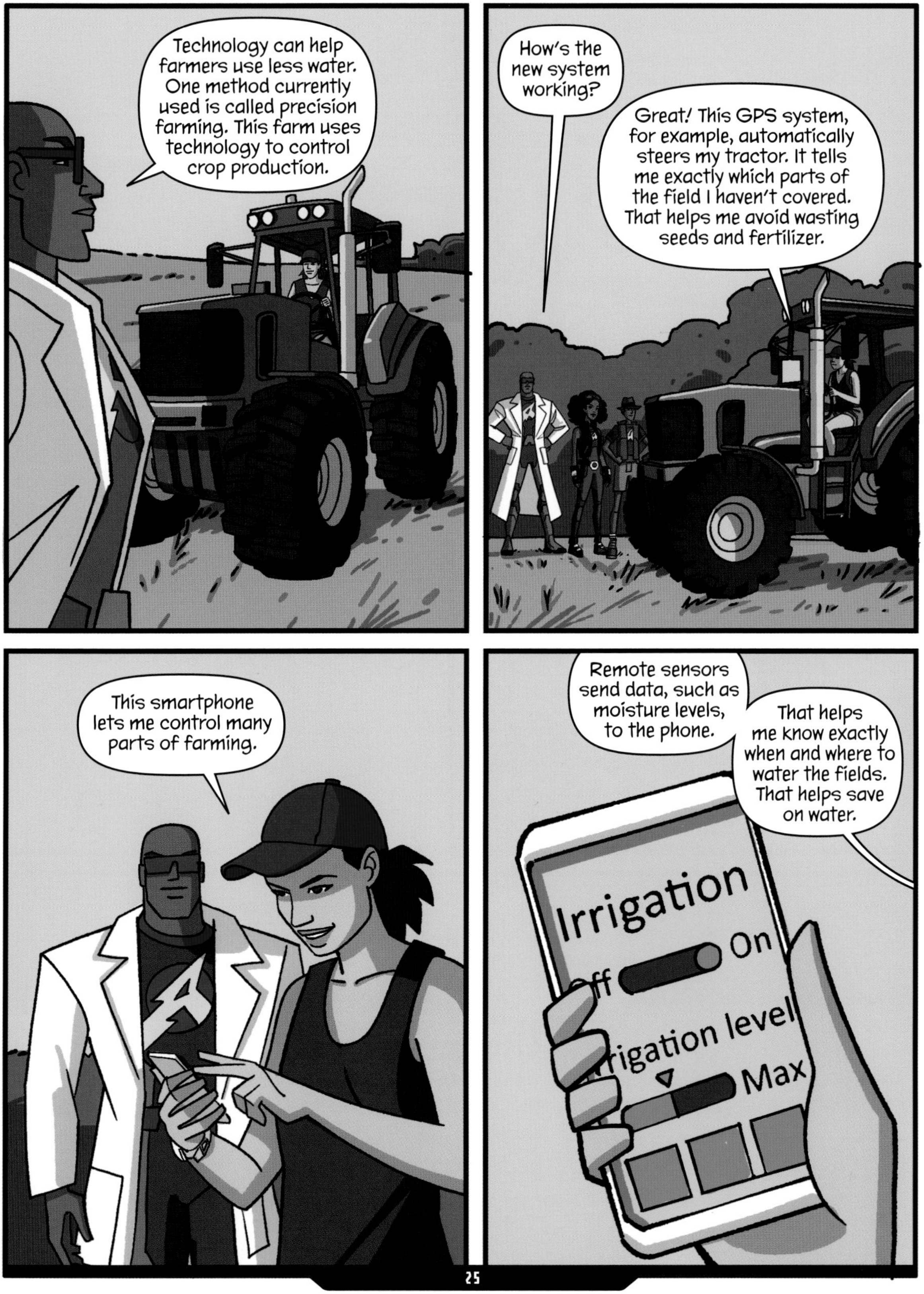
Technology can help farmers use less water. One method currently used is called precision farming. This farm uses technology to control crop production.
How's the new system working?
Great! This GPS system, for example, automatically steers my tractor. It tells me exactly which parts of the field I haven't covered. That helps me avoid wasting seeds and fertilizer.
This smartphone lets me control many parts of farming.
Remote sensors send data, such as moisture levels, to the phone.
That helps me know exactly when and where to water the fields. That helps save on water.
Irrigation
On
Irrigation level
Max

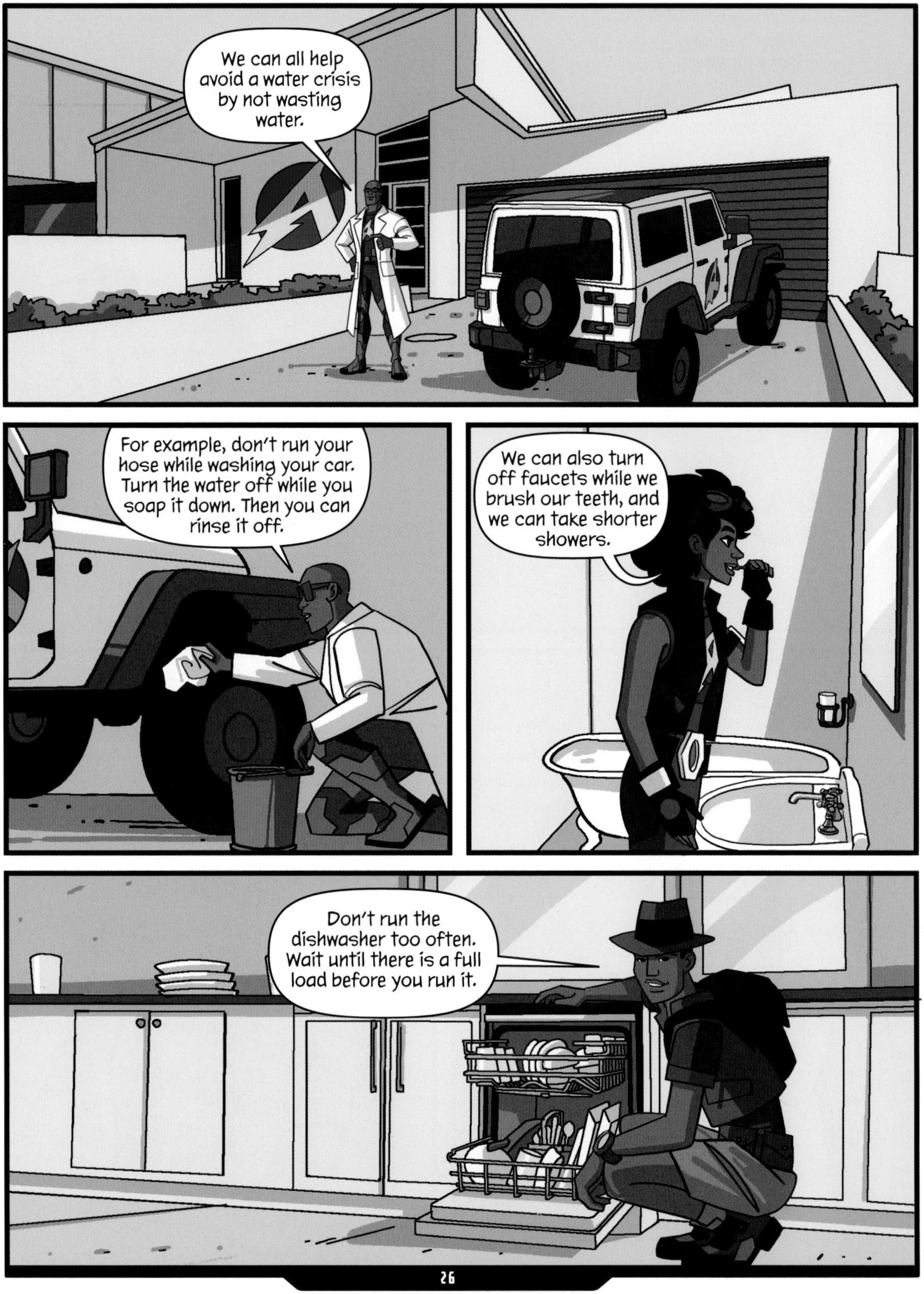
We can all help avoid a water crisis by not wasting water.
For example, don't run your hose while washing your car. Turn the water off while you soap it down. Then you can rinse it off.
We can also turn off faucets while we brush our teeth, and we can take shorter showers.
Don't run the dishwasher too often. Wait until there is a full load before you run it.

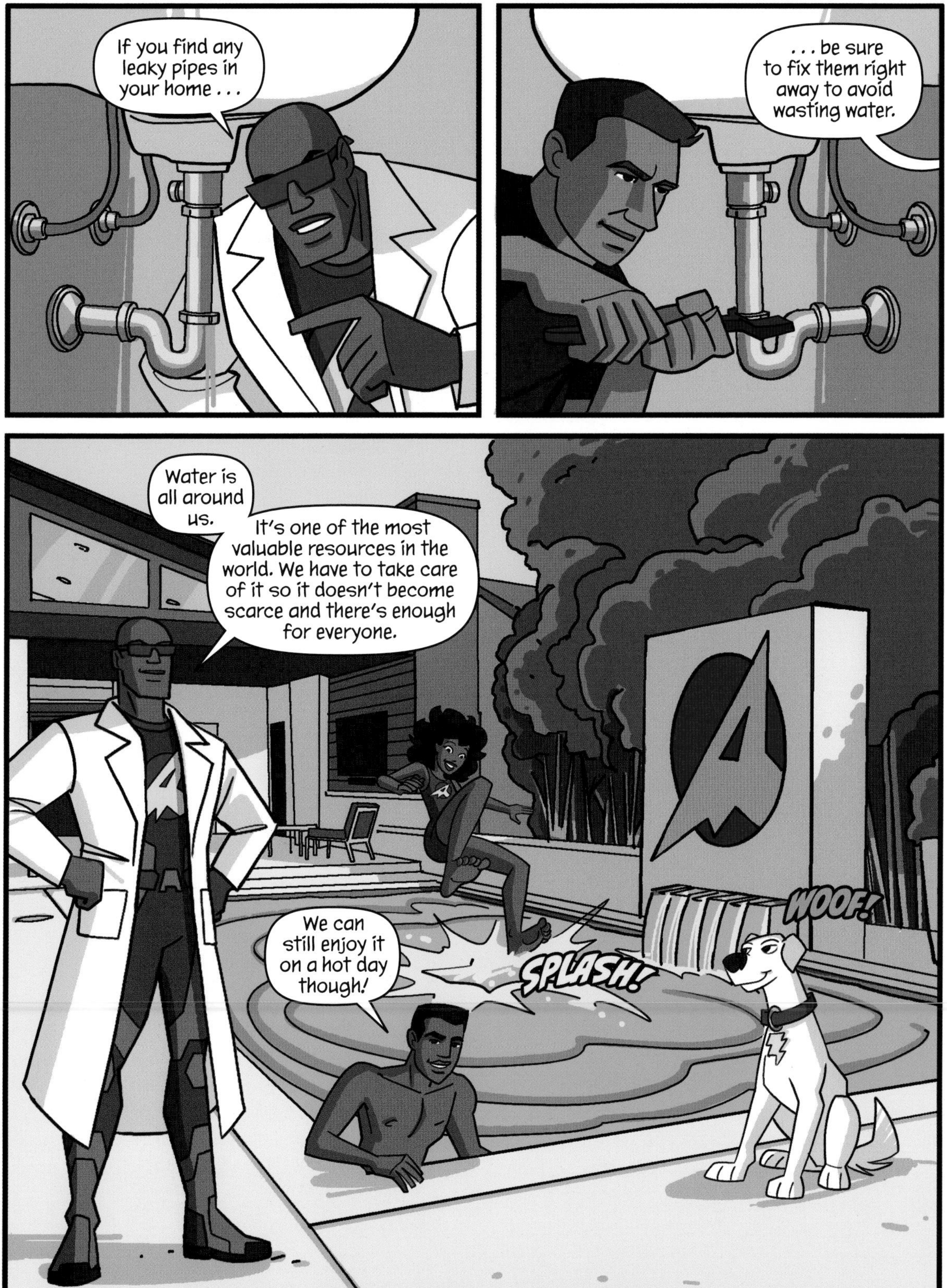
If you find any leaky pipes in your home . . .
. . . be sure to fix them right away to avoid wasting water.
Water is all around us.
It's one of the most valuable resources in the world. We have to take care of it so it doesn't become scarce and there's enough for everyone.
We can still enjoy it on a hot day though!
SPLASH!
WOOF!

TEN INTERESTING FACTS ABOUT WATER

1. The human brain is 75 percent water.

2. People can live for about a month without food. But we can live only three or four days without water.

3. How much does water weigh? About 8 pounds (3.6 kilograms) per gallon.

4. A jellyfish is mostly water—95 percent!

5. NASA has discovered frozen water (ice) on the moon.

6. Water is the only substance on Earth that naturally occurs as a solid, a liquid, and a gas.

7. Water has been recycling on Earth for millions of years. It's possible we're sipping some of the same water that the dinosaurs drank!

8. Over 13 million U.S. homes have private wells instead of using city water supplies.

9. The average human body is about 60 percent water.

10. During an average 5-minute shower, a person uses about 12.5 gallons (47 l) of water.

WHY WE SOMETIMES BOIL WATER

City water is constantly tested to make sure it's safe. Sometimes a drop in water pressure at a treatment facility can cause problems. When the pressure drops, water stays in the pipes longer, which could allow bacteria to grow in the pipes. If this happens, the city will issue a "boil water notice." Residents need to take safety precautions until the water is safe again.

If your city sends out a boil water notice:

- Boil tap water for at least one minute before brushing your teeth, drinking it, or cooking with it. Or use bottled water instead. Be sure to give safe water to your pets too.
- Use hand sanitizer after washing your hands with soap and tap water.
- It's okay to take a shower or bath, but don't swallow the water.
- Doing laundry during a boil water notice is fine.

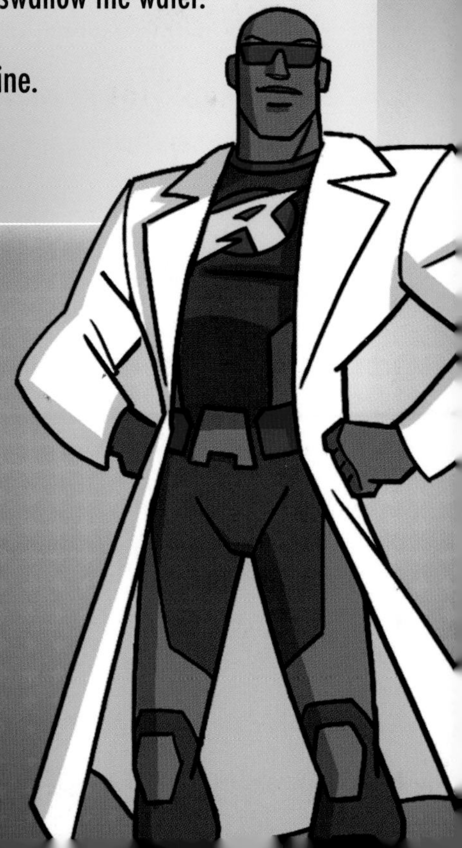

GLOSSARY

aquifer (AH-kwuh-fuhr)—an underground formation that contains ground water

bacteria (bak-TEER-ee-uh)—one-celled, microscopic organisms that exist everywhere in nature; some bacteria cause disease

coagulation (koh-ag-yuh-LAY-shuhn)—the process in which small particles of a substance stick together to form larger clumps

contaminated (kuhn-TAM-uh-nay-tuhd)—dirty or unfit for use

drought (DROUT)—a long period of weather with little to no rainfall

environmental (en-vahy-ruhn-MEN-tuhl)—relating to the natural world

evaporate (i-VAP-uh-rayt)—to change from a liquid to a vapor or a gas

flocculation (flok-yuh-LAY-shuhn)—the process of sediments clumping together to form a larger mass

habitat (HAB-uh-tat)—the natural place and conditions in which an animal or plant lives

irrigation (ihr-uh-GAY-shuhn)—the process of supplying water to crops using a system of pipes or channels

molecule (MOL-uh-kyool)—the atoms that make up the smallest unit of a substance

pesticide (PES-tuh-sahyd)—a poisonous chemical used for killing insects, rats, or other organisms

precision farming (pri-SIZH-uhn FARM-ing)—a type of farming that uses strict management of resources

sediment (SED-uh-muhnt)—bits of sand, mud, and other matter that settle at the bottom of a liquid

READ MORE

Flynn, Riley. *Water Isn't Wasted! How Does Water Become Safe to Drink?*
North Mankato, MN: Capstone Press, 2019.

Hughes, Susan. *Walking for Water: How One Boy Stood Up for Gender Equality.*
Toronto, ON: Kids Can Press, 2021.

Knutson, Julie. *Flint Water Crisis.* Ann Arbor, MI: Cherry Lake Publishing, 2021.

INTERNET SITES

Generation Genius: Water Cycle
generationgenius.com/videolessons/water-cycle-video-for-kids/

NASA Climate Kids: 10 Interesting Things About Water
climatekids.nasa.gov/10-things-water/

Water Footprint Calculator
watercalculator.org

INDEX

ABOUT THE AUTHOR

Myra Faye Turner is a New Orleans-based poet and author. She has written for grownups, but prefers writing for young readers. She has written two dozen nonfiction books for children and young adults, covering diverse topics like politics, the Apollo moon landing, edible insects, and U.S. history. When she's not writing, she spends her days reading, napping, and drinking coffee.